Good Girls Hidden Sins

Shining the Light on the Darkness

CHARITY DERA

Copyright ©2018 by Charity Dera. All rights reserved.

Good Girls Hidden Sins. Printed in the United States of America.

No portion of this book may be reproduced, stored in a retrieval system, or transmitted in any form or by any means except for brief quotations in printed reviews without the prior written permission of Charity Dera.

Unless otherwise indicated, all scripture quotations are taken from the Holy Bible, English Standard Version, The Message Version, New American Standard Bible, New International Version, and New Living Translation.

Interior/Exterior Graphic Design by Karolyne Roberts

ISBN – 978-0-9970264-0-5

TABLE OF CONTENTS

Introduction 6

1 Good Girls 9

2 Hidden Sins 13

3 Pride 16

4 Lust 45

5 Idleness 73

6 Cowardice 94

7 Doubt 120

8 Irritability 141

9 The Gospel 148

10 Rise & Shine 172

Notes 175

Thank You 178

INTRODUCTION

Hi. My name is Charity, and from the surface—many people would consider me a "good girl."

It was never my intention to be labeled as such, the title just sort of—evolved. It came along with the territory of being nice and sweet to people. All the while, I just wanted my teachers to see something in me. I wanted my family to be proud of me. I wanted my peers to approve of me. In essence, I had this insatiable craving to be validated by any means possible. So—I did what any kid craving affirmation would do. I made good grades, never got a disciplinary referral, always said "please" and "thank you" and tried to obey my parents to the best of my ability.

I even used my so-called "good girl" reputation for my own selfish gratification. I mean—people were already using that phrase to define me anyway, so, why not take full-fledged advantage of its perks? This mentality began at a young age. I recall going on a restroom break in second grade and suggesting to the other girls that we play hide and seek—*inside the restroom* (I know...not the most sanitary idea but hey, I was 7). Before the game was over, I slipped out of the restroom almost simultaneously as my teacher barged in. Everyone got into trouble except for me. As the ringleader of this poorly devised (not to mention shady) operation, I thought that fleeing from the scene would somehow make up for my ill-suited behavior.

Using my good girl reputation to my advantage continued as the years progressed. In my seventh-grade reading class, a male peer and I got into some type of minor dispute before class started. I responded by swinging my purse at him (clearly it didn't take much for emotions to heighten at 12). Consequently, the strap of my purse snapped. As my teacher entered the room and noticed the apparent dysfunction, she asked us what happened and believed my dishonest alibi over his—because in her words, "who was she to believe?" He was sent to the principal's office immediately.

Though my behavior in these recollections may appear to be innocent, adolescent flaws that one might potentially outgrow, they stemmed from deep-rooted heart issues that were casually swept under the rug. Contrary to my belief, I couldn't just minimize my behavior by merely bandaging up the ugly parts of myself and placing the blame on other people. No matter how hard I tried, I couldn't make it better, nor could I take away the insistent guilt that ate away at me. Even when everyone else was pleased with my facade—I knew subconsciously that their approval would never be enough. A bandage just wasn't sufficient to cover the multitude of sins I had committed. I needed a much stronger remedy. I needed God.

GOOD GIRLS

"Therefore I tell you, her sins, which are many, are forgiven— for she loved much. But he who is forgiven little, loves little."
(Luke 7:47, ESV)

"She has forgiven many, many sins, and so she is very, very grateful. If the forgiveness is minimal the gratitude is minimal."
(Luke 7:47, MSG)

After having read a passage from the book, *Tortured for Christ* by Reverend Richard Wurmbrand, I saw this scripture from a totally different perspective than the many times I had read it in the past. Having endured the evils of communism for fourteen years in a prison, Wurmbrand had been tortured, mocked and persecuted for proclaiming the gospel of Jesus Christ in Romania. Even after enduring such traumatizing experiences, he had this to say about his adversaries: "I have personally known converted Communists. I myself was a militant atheist in my youth. Converted atheists and Communists love Christ much because they have sinned very much."[1] Wow! That statement resonated with me. Jesus forgave Wurmbrand for *all* of his sins, even for totally denying His existence earlier in Wurmbrand's lifetime. Wurmbrand loved much because he was forgiven much and even chose to love those who persecuted him. I believe this love that he had for people who had been overtaken by social evils derived from genuine empathy. I am convinced that at some point, he realized, being a converted atheist, he could have very well been in his persecutor's shoes.

Then I asked myself, "How much do I love Christ?" I answered, "I love Jesus, I attend church, I serve, I pray, I'm repentant." I even said, "Jesus and I have a pretty good relationship." But would I go so far as to die for the sake of the One who died for me? In theory, my answer was yes. In my heart, I knew that although I would probably die for Christ's sake, I was not too sure if I would do it cheerfully—even knowing that I would be uniting with Him in His sufferings. Would I resent God for allowing me to suffer? Would I be bitter? I honestly don't know, I have never been placed in that predicament but it was definitely something to think about. Then, I thought that like so many others in persecuted countries, Wurmbrand was so faithful and willing to die for the faith because he loved Christ *that* much. It was the least he could do after all that Jesus did for him. I realized that it was very possible that my love wasn't as vigorous as Wurmbrand's because I didn't recognize the weight of my sins. If you owe much and are relieved of your debt, you are prone to show more gratitude than someone who is pardoned from a smaller debt.

The difference between me and Wurmbrand isn't that he was more sinful than I was— in the eyes of a Holy God, we were both offensive. Psalm 53:3 (which Paul also references in Romans) plainly states, "Everyone has turned away, all have become corrupt; there is no one who does good, not even one" (NIV). The difference between me and Wurmbrand is simple.

Wurmbrand recognized his sin and the weight of that sin more than I did, and as a result, seemingly, his pores innately spewed out unadulterated worship unto God. Though our sins bear different consequences, the sins remain. While Wurmbrand can be seen as the sinful woman who anointed Jesus in Luke chapter 7, I was the Pharisee spectating. My sin was more implicit, thus, blinding me from the hypocrisy that dwelled inside of me. While my sins may not have carried popularly recognized stigmas, it did not mean that they were any less repulsive to God. We can agree that communism and atheism are obvious evils in society. However, we often forget about faithlessness and pride; are these sins any less egregious to God? No, not necessarily. Granted, God is a righteous Judge, and can administer justice any way He chooses, however, whether it was by pride or atheism—we've all turned our backs on God. This is the plague of the "good girl" or anyone who deems themselves a "good" person. Goodness in society is relative and subjective. Christ's goodness, however, is concrete and objective. His goodness is the only one that counts because it is cosigned by God. Thus, His goodness is warranted. This is *Good Girls Hidden Sins.*

HIDDEN SINS

"For all that is secret will eventually be brought into the open, and everything that is concealed will be brought to light and made known to all." (Luke 8:17, NLT)

"For everyone who does evil hates the Light, and does not come to the Light for fear that his deeds will be exposed. But he who practices the truth comes to the Light, so that his deeds may be manifested as having been wrought in God."
(John 3:20-21, NASB)

Hiding has been man's innate response to sin ever since it entered the world. As Adam confronted Almighty God after his deliberate disobedience, he had nothing more to show for himself than the shame and embarrassment of sin's residue. Consequently, he felt compelled to cover his shame with fig leaves just to vainly esteem himself as presentable. Truth is, he felt overexposed when susceptible to this piercing, righteous, glorious Light—that is, God. Retreating to the darkness did nothing more than coddle the full-grown sin that had already been birthed inside of him. Yet, in the moment, this darkness provided Adam with a false sense of security. Little did he know that the very Light that he had been retreating from would be the same Light that would later save him.

Sadly, not much has changed since Adam's day. In fact, humanity's diagnosis (in my opinion) has worsened. Some of us don't even feel compelled to hide the shame of our sins anymore—we'd rather boast in our filth and bask in the glory of acceptance from our sinful counterparts (Romans 1:32).

Nevertheless, as a "good girl," hiding had always been my reaction after I sinned. I've always been terrified that if people knew who I *really* was, they wouldn't want any dealings with me. Allowing people into that dark alleyway of my heart where only God and I resided was never an option—until now.

The weightiness of living a secret life in sin can be burdensome, especially for us "good girls." So who will intercede for us? Who will erase the guilt and shame? Who will save us from judgment? Who will transform our wicked hearts, enabling us to receive the Light with clarity, instead of intrinsic rebellion? Jesus will. He's the only reason why I'm not afraid of exposing my filth today. It is for His glory and your edification that I write these words. Brace yourself for the journey "good girl"; we are about to approach the road of hidden sins.

PRIDE

God speak through me!
This is for Your glory
If it happens to make me look
like a better Christian in the process,
I will attribute it to Your glory—
Instead of my pride.
Instead of my selfish ambition.
Instead of admitting that my heart
is pretty messed up, I'll say
"Praise God."
But did I really want it for myself,
did I want You to praise me?
To glorify me?
Something that only belongs to You, God.
If that's in fact true then
I have become my own idol.

You see, Jesus only performed miracles to glorify the Father.
If the people see the connection
between Jesus and God, they must be related.
And if people confess that Jesus is the Son of God
And repent of their ways
they are now saved.
Miracles are so much more than making the vessel look good.
It's a bit more serious than that.
It's about God's glory.
So maybe God's not performing miracles in my life

18 Pride

because He knows I'm going to attempt to steal
His glory for myself.
As if it's possible...

Real glory is this:
Downgrading Your residence
to exchange Your glory for
a suit of flesh that reeks of human.

As a baby, You submitted yourself
to Your parents.
Always obeying and respecting
never sinning.
Though You made them with Your own hands.

With those hands You became a carpenter.
Those same hands healed the blind,
touched the lame,
cured the demon-possessed
and no one even cared.

The humanity that You were in pursuit of
could care less
about You and Your ministry.

They were so wrapped up in their glory
That they crucified You

Because they got insecure when You told them
who You were.

The Son of God.
They couldn't wrap their minds around
Your glory.
So they made their own.
If only they knew they were instruments
In Your holistic plan
of saving humankind.

If only they knew that You laid down Your life
No man took it from You
or Your glory.

So when You resurrected
I bet they felt real dumb.
Holding the Only One hostage
who came to set them free.

But instead of condemning them,
You loved them.
And graciously
Gave them salvation…
that's glory.

So my take away from that story is

Pride

That I'm them and they're me
So I guess I drove the nails in Your hands to that tree
When I wanted all of that glory for me.

The precious thing about us
Is that God still uses us for His glory.
Even when we try to take it for ourselves.
He's so in control He still gets it all,
because glory can't go where glory doesn't belong.

"Better to be lowly in spirit along with the oppressed than to share plunder with the proud."
(Proverbs 16:19, NIV)

Pride is a sin that is often overlooked in American culture. It's possible that pride has become so widely accepted—some might not even consider it a sin. We hear phrases like "school pride," "black pride," and "gay pride" daily. Fathers teach their sons to have pride in who they are and where they came from. Men who are prideful are sometimes considered as more masculine than others and conceivably more attractive to women. Some rappers make their living based on predominantly prideful lyrics. Consumers typically advocate these lyrics because they are enticed by a beat. Many intellectuals have the tendency to pride themselves in their finite knowledge, which consequently blinds them from recognizing their own foolish capacities. From the outside looking in, it appears as if society bathes in pride. Yes, bathes. We lather in it to cleanse ourselves from our insecurities. In doing so, we put on a false persona by only displaying the cropped and edited images we want everyone to see. God forbid we expose our actual flaws and failures to illuminate the vulnerable, true parts of ourselves. God forbid we recognize these flaws and bring glory to someone greater than ourselves in the process. God forbid we recognize that this life is about more than just us...

All About ~~Me~~ Him

Have you ever been so caught up in your own imperfections and dilemmas that you seemed to forget that there's an entire universe that exists outside of you? I certainly have, partially because it's so easy to adopt this "me" mentality in such a self-involved society. Literally, the universe is occupied by billions of galaxies; we as humans are only exposed to one, the Milky Way Galaxy. Within the outer reaches of the Milky Way Galaxy lies our solar system. It is only at the point of entering this solar system that human beings are even capable of viewing some of the sky's landmarks with the naked eye. Our micro-perspective of the sun, stars, and moon don't begin to do the rest of the solar system justice.

Similar to our micro-perspective of the universe, we can also adopt the same isolated construction of our very lives. With the naked eye, it appears as if our lives were granted to us merely for our own edification and satisfaction. Owning this mentality is inhibiting. If our lives were just about us, then any series of situations and circumstances could easily wreck our livelihood. But if our lives point to someone greater, nothing and no one could ever snatch the overarching purpose our lives were designed to fulfill. God's Word challenges our narrow-minded micro-perspectives with His all-encompassing macro-perspective. We disadvantage ourselves by behaving as if the world revolves around our own finite life stories. Instead, we ought to realize that we merely exist as characters in God's supreme, epic story. Understanding the implications of pride and seeking to eliminate it in our hearts can help us see this macro picture that God is trying to convey to us more clearly.

How God Views Pride

Pride may appear ordinary and minuscule to us, but God loathes it. He has made that clear in Scripture. "To fear the Lord is to hate evil; I hate pride and arrogance, evil behavior and perverse speech" (Proverbs 8:13, NIV). Humans have been prideful since the beginning of the age. Adam and Eve gave birth to sin when they listened to the enemy's lie—thinking they would acquire God's knowledge by eating from the tree of the knowledge of good and evil, even after God had distinctly instructed Adam not to (Genesis 3). In that moment, they had esteemed their own finite wisdom above the instruction of an infinitely wise God.

Sarai (Sarah) could have allowed pride and fear to consume her when she permitted Hagar to sleep with her husband out of a potential insecurity regarding her inability to conceive. Even after God had promised her husband Abram (Abraham) that he would have descendants as numerous as the stars, she prematurely took matters into her own hands instead of patiently trusting in God's promises. It seems as if all throughout the Scriptures we see this pattern of man exhibiting pride, man consequently falling as a result of his pride, and the Word of God prevailing over it all.

Humility

Humility is very necessary when counteracting pride. However, this is no easy venture. Humbling ourselves, or better yet—asking God to humble us, obliges us to be just like Jesus. How is it that the Son of God—this all encompassing, all knowing, omnipotent Creator of the universe, is able to come to Earth in the first place? Have you ever taken a moment to think about that? He left His heavenly throne to dwell within this sinful, tainted earth—His very own footstool (Isaiah 66:1) so that He could sacrifice His life in order to reconcile us back to the Father. His holiness and splendor were confined within the womb of a woman. A woman He created. He humbled Himself to the extent that He allowed His parents Joseph and Mary to take care of Him as a child when He was sufficient all by Himself. Though He has all the riches and glory imaginable, He lived a life as a poor carpenter in Nazareth. A town in which "nothing good has ever come from" (John 1:46). As an adult, He made His dwelling among us but the very world that He created did not recognize Him. His own people didn't even receive Him (John 1:10-11). He endured persecution, mocking, rejection, and a torture-filled crucifixion from His very own creation. The beautiful thing is, He knew what He was getting into in advance. He knew he would be denied three times by His close friend and disciple Peter. He already knew Judas was going to betray Him with a kiss. Yet, He still did it—all because He loves us. He who knew no sin became sin for us—the very thing He hates! The only one who could pass judgment on us came not to judge but to save. The One whom we should be serving came not to be served but to serve. If Jesus could be so radically humble, what makes us think so highly of ourselves?

Why Good Girls Fall Victim to Pride

It is unnatural to constantly be reminded of how "good" you are, being that as fallen human beings, we are unqualified to be described in such a manner. If someone is constantly being reminded of supposed "goodness," a goodness by which they are incapable of obtaining, in my opinion, it will be extremely difficult for that person not to have a swollen sense of self. Don't get me wrong, there's nothing wrong with receiving compliments. The issue at hand is that many of us who have been categorized as good girls ingest compliments, especially compliments that are by nature, disingenuously toxic. For example, if someone uses statements like "You're perfect," or "You're so innocent," to describe someone whom they perceive to be "good," those compliments are not so complimentary after all because they are inherently false. There is no one who has achieved perfection, nor is there anyone who has inherited innocence in any capacity, apart from Christ. In an attempt to use those compliments casually, people can mistakenly esteem others in a manner that should only be used for the exaltation of God alone. Or perhaps consider an ordinary compliment such as "You're so intelligent!" There's nothing wrong with the statement in and of itself. This type of compliment is not inherently toxic and could be used for edification purposes. However, if one ever gets to the point that they uphold the value of other people's words over God's Word, that is an equation set up for failure. Subconsciously, the good girl could potentially walk around with a false sense of humility by accrediting her intelligence, for example, to God. As soon as she begins to do poorly, however, she may start condemning herself about her performance. Ultimately, revealing that her confidence derived from herself instead of God. "I'm supposed to have this reputation and my performance doesn't amount to what people think I am. What do I do? Maybe I'm not so smart after all," she might mutter to herself. Immediately, her self-esteem spirals downward. The fall didn't come because the good girl was confident, it came because she lifted herself so high (by esteeming herself in herself) that she had nowhere to go but right back down. When we are properly grounded (by esteeming ourselves in God's Word) there's nowhere to go but up. The only way to get to the ground is to be humbled. Either we stay on the ground and humble ourselves by choice, or God will humble us by force. Personally, I much prefer the first option. "Pride goes before destruction, a haughty spirit before a fall" (Proverbs 16:18, NIV). The more prideful we are, the harder we will inevitably fall. Anyone in his or her right mind would prefer to fall out of a tree versus a skyscraper, though either option prescribes its own dose of pain. Pride can easily grow into a skyscraper if we allow it, and will eventually lead to our destruction.

For the Christ follower, pride also has the tendency to twist our mentalities, enabling us to sometimes think that we have arrived—giving us the false assurance that there is nothing left to work on. These are the times that spending time with Christ is so very imperative. He shows us our imperfections while illuminating His splendor. Yet in the midst of His superiority and authority, He never demeans us—instead, He builds our esteem back up, replacing our faulty foundation with Himself. However, if we never come to God, but we act as if we have it all together, we place ourselves in compromising situations. We become self-righteous. Acknowledging the plague of sin in our lives shows God's almighty power to wash us clean with His one and only sacrifice. There's a difference between seeking perfection for the sake of our reputation versus seeking Jesus for the sake of our redemption.

The "good girl" is also susceptible to fall victim to pride because nobody tells her about herself! People may mistake her haughty spirit for confidence and dignity. They can also deem her lack of transparency as perfection. Though we cannot control what others think of us, if the "good girl" is equally convinced that these characteristics are true based on a façade-fueled demeanor and suppression of truth, she cosigns with darkness and refuses to live in God's light. "Good girls" (just like anyone else) must hold themselves accountable to God as well as other godly counsel.

Good Girls, Pride & The Gospel

We hear this concept of the "good" girl, and the "good" person all the time, but is being good really going to get you into heaven? Many think it will. Feed the homeless. Be nice to people. Give to the poor. Apply a couple of bible verses every now and then. Be positive. Excel in your career. Have good energy. Repeat. Many individuals have adopted these philosophies. Though at face value there is nothing innately wrong with the aforementioned list, without full submission and faith in Jesus, these attitudes will not breed righteousness. Typically, as humans, we have the habit of comparing our wrongdoing with someone else's—weighing the two offenses on a balance scale and hoping that our sin weighs less. Having these considerations furthers the justification of our rebellion against God. It is true, we may appear righteous compared to someone else, but how are we looking in comparison to Christ? By comparing one human offense to another, it's as if we decided to collect a heaping amount of used tampons and deemed that filthy pile clean in our own sight. Many would consider us mentally ill for refusing to believe what is blatantly true. Similarly, to fathom that God is pleased with filthy deeds that have been egotistically deemed "righteous," is purely illogical (Isaiah 64:6). Being that God is holy, He is never pleased with unrighteousness. So when comparing my offense with another person's and simultaneously convincing myself that my filthy rag looks nice in association with their filthy rag,

I'm being utterly ridiculous! They're both filthy! That's the kind of mentality that we have when labeling one another "good." In God's eyes, we're both dying. Our sin equals death (Romans 6:23). Point. Blank. Period. Devastating, right?

That's where the good news comes in! God knew how filthy we were so He sent His one and only Son, Jesus, to cleanse us from our iniquities. God being just and fair couldn't just cleanse us and keep it moving. We needed to somehow pay for our sins and the only wage for our sins is eternal death. Sin is that serious of an offense. So, instead of having us pay this penalty ourselves, God sent us His only Son—a perfect Redeemer (Jesus) who was fully man and fully God all at the same time. Jesus came to take the death penalty that we all deserve by laying down His life on a cross. The great thing about this good news, is that Jesus ultimately beat death by resurrecting on the third day after He was crucified. He not only paid the death sentence that we deserved once and for all, but through Him we're no longer enemies of God! Now when God looks at us He doesn't see our sin, but the blood of His Son, which is perfect and without blemish (Hebrews 10:10). Jesus paved the way so that we can have life and relationship with God for all of eternity. God's demonstration of this elaborate plan to save us shows His great love and pursuit of humanity.

You're probably wondering what pride has to do with the gospel. Pride blinds our eyes so that we won't see how sinful we actually are. Pride makes us believe that we don't need saving. Pride can, with subtleness, deceive—causing many to reject God and His gift of salvation. Some may respond to these truths in saying, "I never rejected God! I go to church on Sundays, I serve, I give!" But Jesus says, "Many will say to me on that day, 'Lord, Lord, did we not prophesy in your name, and in your name drive out demons, and in your name perform many miracles?' And then I will tell them plainly, 'I never knew you. Away from me, you evildoers!'" (Matthew 7:22-23, NIV). A person's actions should bear fruit and testify to knowing Jesus, not just merely knowing about Him. Jesus Himself desires to *know* us—He wants our hearts which should ultimately fuel our obedience. By having this mentality of doing things on our own and living lives solely for our own pleasure, we deceive ourselves if we ever thought that in acting this way God is pleased. Pride will con us into believing that it is sufficient to posture Jesus as a supplement rather than our ultimate necessity.

After all, pride could be perceived as a main motivator of some prosperity teaching. Sometimes, we desire so badly to please ourselves and do what makes us happy that we merely use God for the sake of earthly pleasures. Though we may be basking in our prosperity, wealth, and popularity now, what a shame that without repentance this life will literally be the best life some will ever live. What's so unfortunate is that this mentality is so prevalent in the American culture. For the sake of achieving the "American Dream," some will do anything—even forsake their souls. What about God's dream? Sadly, some will never care to ask due to preoccupation with their own ambitions, lusts and gratifications. Some individuals are so consumed with themselves that they refuse to open God's Word, or worse—*defend* their perverted motives with God's Word. Many neglect their need for salvation by living this way. Jesus says, "Blessed are the poor in spirit, for theirs is the kingdom of heaven" (Matthew 5:3, NIV). The word "blessed" in this text comes from the Greek word *makarios*, which literally means happy. Happy are the poor in spirit, for theirs is the kingdom of heaven. Who are the poor in spirit? People who realize they are sinful and deserving of death. The poor in spirit also understand that Jesus is the only One who can pay the due penalty for their sin sentence. Without Jesus, they are literally dead. Those people who have and live this understanding will inherit the Kingdom of God. The opposite perspective of being poor in spirit is given in Luke's account of the gospel when Jesus says: "But woe to you who are rich, for you have already received your comfort" (Luke 6:24, NIV). Jesus is essentially saying that those who find comfort and security in their riches will be eternally sorrowful. We have a choice to either anchor our faith in our possessions, (and inherently make them our gods) or anchor our faith in the one true living God. By no means is God anti-rich, but He wants to be Lord over your life. He doesn't want to compete with your stuff. He also doesn't want you to vainly esteem yourself as self-sufficient. If He told you to get rid of your possessions and give them to the poor for His glory would you object? (Matthew 19:16-22). He wants your heart—

why else would He die in your place? He wants you to understand that your sin, similar to an illness, is chronic and *will* result in death. He wants you to realize that Jesus took that inevitable death so that you may actually experience true life. What's so sad is that the only life some people actually live is one filled with tragedy, heartache, pain, injustice, and trials. We have our houses, cars, families, possessions, degrees, knowledge, and hobbies—the works. All of those things are nice, but do we even recognize our need for salvation? As Americans, we can sometimes look down on materially impoverished nations, yet many natives of those same countries at least comprehend their utter necessity for God. When everything's good in life it's so easy to discount God and start thinking that *you* make stuff happen, that you are the god of your own life. Why would we ever think to look to God unless we needed Him in the first place? I know I didn't start checking for God until I was in a situation that I couldn't get myself out of in my own power. Romans 3:10-11 states that "There is no one righteous, not even one; there is no one who understands; there is no one who seeks God" (NIV). No one comes to God on his or her own accord. It's God who leads us back to God (John 6:44). He humbles our haughty spirits so that we can realize our spiritually impoverished state without Him. That's how graciously loving God is—He will break us just to heal us.

My Struggle with Pride

I have been subconsciously prideful ever since I can remember. I haven't always acknowledged it. Ironically enough, I believe pride was the very thing that kept me from truly accepting Christ at a young age. Growing up in church and hearing the message of the gospel as a kid didn't really evoke anything inside of me. I desired authentic salvation, but all I found myself caring about was using God to get into heaven. I didn't truly understand the weight of my sin in the first place. Surely, I couldn't comprehend why hell was necessary—for me at least. Murderers and villains made sense, but would God really send *me* to hell? I was just a nice girl who went to school to make good grades. Isn't that what He wanted? And why was it that no one ever encountered God in his or her youth? Was holiness only manufactured for my grandma's generation? Would He allow me to have my fun in my youth so that salvation could at least be "worth it" in my old age?

Ultimately, I wanted to have everything heavenly in eternity while discounting the glorious, almighty God who is life itself. I also didn't understand the concept of praising God forever. I mean who does that? Wouldn't that get boring? I was only using God for what He could give me and not for who He was. Now, I realize that heaven without God is actually called hell, and life without God is a paradox. I found myself coming up empty time and time again because I was in constant pursuit of the creation versus the Creator.

Meanwhile, I lived a worrisome, fearful existence. What does a kid have to worry about you may ask? Absolutely nothing, but I managed to find insignificant things to dwell upon each and every day. I never had peace because in my mind, it all depended on me. I was my own god, after all. I professed the name of Jesus at church, even got "saved" but my heart was left destitute and untransformed. I recall repeating the prayer of repentance all the time just to convince myself that I wasn't going to hell. These prayers became even more repetitive due to the fact that I was terribly paranoid that Jesus was coming back any day and He might leave me in the process—thanks to the movie *Left Behind*. However, this paranoia would have never manifested had I trusted God. I couldn't trust God because I didn't know Him. I knew about Jesus of course, but I honestly didn't feel like I needed Him. Subconsciously, I thought I had to be more sinful before I *really* got saved. But currently, as a "good girl," I was doing fine.

Pride has also revealed itself in my life in the form of insecurity. I used to crave compliments and attention from people because of how insecure I was deep inside. I yearned for people to boost me up and put me on a pedestal just to mask how I really felt internally. In middle school, like most girls, I went through my awkward ugly duckling stage. My head was not proportionate to my body, I had braces (with matching brackets and rubber bands), and of course, I inherited my father's bushy eyebrows. Ugly didn't begin to describe how I felt. Fast forward four years later. I was a sophomore in high school. I was growing into my body, my teeth were straight and I was finally allowed to get my eyebrows arched! My self-esteem went through the roof. Suddenly, boys who didn't even know I existed before were admiring me—it was only natural for me (in my mind) to willingly accept the attention. Pride had me feeling beyond puffed up. Yet, I still hadn't managed to mask the insecurity that was eating me alive day after day.

Vanity

"And you, O desolate one, what do you mean that you dress in scarlet, that you adorn yourself with ornaments of gold, that you enlarge your eyes with paint? In vain you beautify yourself. Your lovers despise you; they seek your life."
(Jeremiah 4:30, ESV)

I have discovered that pride comes in many packages; many that I have had the displeasure of owning. Vanity, in particular, is a byproduct of pride that struck a significant chord in the medley of my past.

Ever since I was a little girl, I was taught that staring at oneself in mirrors was "vain." Yet, no one ever defined vanity for me. My sister would always remind me "don't be vain." I could only assume it to be negative. However, I didn't understand why it held that connotation. Models looked at themselves, women on television seemed to appreciate the way they looked—why did I have to hold a different standard? As the little girl that I was, I didn't think much of it. I really had no reason to be vain at that point; I just wanted to live my six-year-old carefree life.

That didn't last long. My age seemed to have an inverse relationship with my self-esteem. As I grew older, the more insecure I became with how I looked—and felt. I had allowed people's opinions to define me, particularly boys'. These are a few insults I remember hearing from my peers:

> "Are you mute?"
> "Can you read?"
> "Do you have a personality?"
> "Why do you smile so much when your teeth are messed up?"
> "Your face would look so much cleaner if you got your eyebrows done."

Of course, kids will be cruel—but that fact of life didn't help me any. I wanted so badly to be this insanely gorgeous, intelligent girl who just overflowed with popularity. This skewed standard of liveliness and worth became the focal point of my life. Much of my behavior during this time stemmed from my desire to be socially accepted. It appeared as if the older I became, the more deeply rooted my insecurities were—permitting me to become increasingly vain as a result. I had to mask my insecurities somehow. It felt better to deviate the attention of others to my appearance because, to me, my insides were too messy to be exposed. As a result, I subconsciously focused on my appearance excessively, so that people would accept me. From the age of about fifteen forward, I was feeling myself. I was getting my brows waxed regularly, wearing cute clothes (courtesy of my sister's closet), and getting the attention of boys. I was dolled up outwardly, but so empty internally. The nerve I had to consider myself virtuous—as if I knew what true virtue was still appalls me.

Thank God for Facebook, because sometimes I unintentionally repress my memories so much that I almost forget how I used to be. My old photos might not seem like a big deal to other people, but I can see the brokenness written all over them. I was so broken that I can recall harassing my, at the time, ex-boyfriend to look at my high school senior picture album, just so he could tell me how beautiful I was, and ultimately want to be with me again. It's sad how twisted my thoughts were without me even realizing. I was so vain that it was habitual for me to look at my reflection in car windows, department store doors—anything of the sort, I would use. I wasn't being obsessive about my reflection to bask at my beauty either—I was doing it more so to identify the imperfections within me that seemed to be at work at all times. I was yearning to be pacified by any means possible.

Finding my identity in my appearance backfired in college. Before leaving Jacksonville, I made sure to take a selfie of my freshly relaxed, vivacious hair to document the new journey ahead. Lo and behold, the moment I stepped foot in Tampa the humidity was completely on a different level. My hair didn't last two seconds in the summer heat without retracting to a frizz ball. I didn't have money for relaxers (and my dad didn't care to sponsor them away from home), I was too cheap to get my eyebrows done (and carless) and to top it off, I was gaining weight (freshman 15). During that first semester of college, I resorted to wearing jeggings and hoodies because they were the only items in my wardrobe that fit comfortably at the time. All the pride that I had invested in the way I looked slowly disintegrated. So much so, that I didn't even realize I had gained weight until I went home for Thanksgiving break. The absence of a full body mirror in my dorm room had me in complete denial. If I hadn't realized it before, my family was expeditious in delivering the message to me. The point being, that God had me in a place where everything I had aesthetically placed my worth in prior to college, had failed me. It was a place in which I had to confront the inner me, and I wasn't thrilled by any means to do so.

It finally happened—I no longer had a mask to deter people from who I really was. I had ripped that façade off almost as quickly as the weight gain. It was time for true introspection, and my "insides" didn't appear so appealing at first glance. But at least I was authentically myself. It felt good not to have to focus on my appearance as much. At the same time, it was draining being bombarded with a host of insecurities, offenses, and temperaments that had developed over the course of my entire eighteen years of life. I was free from the demands of my mirror, yet, bound to the weight of my baggage.

Only Judge a Book by Its Pages

We've all heard the phrase "don't judge a book by its cover" but I much prefer "only judge a book by its pages." As visual creatures, we're much more apt to read a book after spotting its attractive cover. Lo and behold, after all of that anticipation, we sometimes open that book to discover empty words on stale pages. That was the vain story of my life apart from Christ. However, it's so refreshing to know that God values the substance of a person's pages over the intricacies of their cover. Jesus Himself embodied perfection internally; yet, He didn't even have any physical beauty to attract us to Him on earth (Isaiah 53:2). That just goes to show you how much God cares about appearance. Our hearts are His main objective. It always comforts me to know that what people deem as attractive (beauty, charisma, eloquent words, etc.) don't phase God. He's all the more concerned about our inner, true, eternal beauty. "...The Lord does not look at the things people look at. People look at the outward appearance, but the Lord looks at the heart" (1 Samuel 16:7, NIV).

Sometimes I think to myself, what if I had continued to pride myself in how I looked even after college? Where would I be? If my eyebrows didn't remain perfectly arched 24/7, would I feel like less of a person? Would I have chosen to keep my hair relaxed because that was what society generally deemed as beautiful? Would I have chosen to seek God as fervently as I did, or would I have been too distracted by keeping up my appearance? Though my appearance has taken a backseat to my inner beauty for sure, truth is, I still have my moments when insecurities resurface and I don't feel beautiful. However, in spite of my low moments I'm just truly appreciative that God opened my eyes to what true beauty actually is. Even when pride begins to rise in my heart and I revert to my vain ways—God has a way of bringing me back and showing me that He is far more impressive, radiant, and beautiful than I could ever make myself out to be. Because of that fact, I'd much rather gaze at the infinite awesomeness of Him, rather than restricting my awestruck wonder to a reflection in a mirror.

The Cover Still Entices...

As much as I would like to think inner beauty is all that matters—though God sees the heart, people *still* see my outward appearance. As a result, it is my aim to look decent so that my "cover" will initially entice, but my "pages" are what's going to keep my readers engaged. Before, when vanity was an unrepentant sin in my life, I was literally a slave to people. If society wanted me to look a certain way, I tried my best to accommodate because I needed acceptance and approval. Now that I'm a slave to Christ, my main concern is serving Him, not human opinions. Instead of looking nice to esteem myself, I try to do so to glorify God. Indeed, I believe the external fashioning of my body in a manner that honors the Lord to be vital, since it belongs to Him anyway.

If this shell of a body is worth being clothed and taken care of, how much more imperative is it that my eternal soul be intentionally adorned? The cost to maintain outward beauty could, at most, require a significant monetary contribution. However, having a clean heart is far more valuable than currency. It required an unglamorous sacrifice from an unblemished Savior so that in faith, I could stand blameless before a holy God. At the end of the day, I want my redeemed heart to reflect the radiance of Christ so much so, that it easily transfers externally.

Discouraged by Pride?

"They came to Capernaum. When he was in the house, he asked them, 'What were you arguing about on the road?' But they kept quiet because on the way they had argued about who was the greatest.
Sitting down, Jesus called the Twelve and said, 'Anyone who wants to be first must be the very last, and the servant of all.' He took a little child whom he placed among them. Taking the child in his arms, he said to them, 'Whoever welcomes one of these little children in my name welcomes me; and whoever welcomes me does not welcome me but the one who sent me.'"
(Mark 9:33-37, NIV)

Acknowledge It - Mark 9:33-34

Jesus already knows your thoughts. He knows the committal of pride before it even manifests. Confess it to Him, confess it to yourself. Admit the sin so that you can be healed. Sometimes, we keep quiet like the disciples in verse 34 because we're ashamed and embarrassed. Although confession can be the hardest thing for us to do at times because it exposes us, we can find security and comfort in knowing that Jesus didn't come to condemn us for our sin, but to save us from it (Luke 19:10).

Be Humbled - Mark 9:35

Being a servant will humble us inevitably. Jesus is the ultimate example of this. By first sitting down while talking to the disciples in this passage, Jesus' very posture illustrates His intention. He's showing them literally what the greatest looks like—someone who serves all, placing himself last. Now, let's not get confused, we can't manipulate mere works as devices to achieve "humility." Just because we serve doesn't mean we're humble. Putting yourself last just so you can say you're the first isn't a genuine reason to be last in the first place. Let Jesus check your heart by humbly praying and seeking His Word before serving in any capacity. You want your intentions and motives to be pure.

Trust in Jesus, Not Yourself - Mark 9:36-37

Jesus wants us to welcome the little children. Why? Because children are needy, they have nothing and require everything. Jesus wants us to be dependent on Him. Why else? Because children are sometimes considered powerless and marginalized within society. For what other reason would we possibly do this? Because children have faith (Matthew 18:3)! They're not afraid to ask for their wants and needs and do so unashamedly. If something goes wrong, most children have this full assurance that their parents will fix the issue at hand. If they accidentally break a vase, for example, although there might be consequences for disobeying instructions, a gracious parent is always there to pick up the broken pieces. It's unfortunate that when we get older, this mentality seems to dissipate. We get so caught up in life that we often forget that even though it's often considered unattractive to be clingy to our parents at a mature age, God actually desires and cherishes this eternal bond between Him and His children. He wants us to revel in His consistent character—always trusting in Him because He cares. Even when we accidentally (and purposefully for that matter) shatter life's vases by going against God's righteous rules and sinning—He is more than faithful to restore our broken pieces for our good and His glory.

"Not to us, O Lord, not to us, but to your name give glory, for the sake of your steadfast love and your faithfulness!"
(Psalm 115:1, ESV)

LUST

A Thing Called Lust

In my weakest moment
You were there
Taunting my spirit, luring me...

To a place where
I was paralyzed
A slave to my flesh,
Petrified!
How could I let my curiosity
Get the best of me
Going and going
That was the end of me.

The death of me.
The rest of me.
He had tested me,
And I didn't care,
I had turned my back, parts bare.
Everything premeditated in my mind
Had gone down
And that was fine.

Until it hit me and I was all alone.
To face my sin,

Mind blown.
How could I let myself be the girl
Who defiled her temple
Without a care.
Love relinquished,
To a man impaired.

Though conviction was there
I brushed it aside
Dove into that pool
Full of lies.
I said stop.
But persistence left
A faint whisper,
Tuned out, deaf.

I refuse to be in lust again
Christ has redeemed His child, revoked her sin.
Grace at its best, I no longer die.
He did that already for you and I.
Purified, no need to cry
I've been renewed
My love is alive, no longer skewed
By a thing called lust.

Lust. Love. Who really knows the difference anymore?

For a long time, I didn't. As a result, lust became permissible. Getting aroused by a sex scene in a movie was okay every now and again. Undressing dudes in my head was normal. Entertaining perverted dreams kept me thriving. As long as I didn't have intercourse, I thought I was okay. As long as I didn't act on my desires, I found them justifiable and natural. I couldn't have been any further from the truth.

Defining Lust

But I tell you that anyone who looks at a woman lustfully has already committed adultery with her in his heart.
(Matthew 5:28, NIV)

Lust is typically defined in a sexual context, however this word can also be applied in other contexts. For example, having a strong desire for food in a manner that competes with my affections and/or desires for God can also be considered lust. Though God has graciously given me my taste buds to enjoy food and partake in its inherent yummy-ness, if my desire for food ever contends with the love I should have for God, yummy-ness can quickly transform into idolatry, with food being the object of my lust. The word *epithymeo,* which is the Greek word used for "lust" in Matthew 5:28, literally means "to turn upon a thing; to have a desire for, long for, desire; to lust after, covet (of those who seek things forbidden)." However, since the

Scriptures typically speak about lust in reference to a sexual covetousness and/or desire, for purposes of this chapter, I will also be referencing it from that lens.

    In order to properly unpack the definition for lust previously given, I find it necessary to understand the context of Matthew 5:28. This verse is interjected within the midst of Jesus' Sermon on the Mount, where He masterfully expounds upon the essential relationship between "law" and "heart" and proves the legitimacy of the law in doing so. It is at this mountain where He lavishes divine insight, showing that the Law of Moses surpasses mere behavioral parameters but instead seeps deep to the heart of the matter—ultimately foreshadowing how He Himself will fulfill the law, not abolish it. In doing so, He speaks openly, giving mind blowing revelations with each Word uttered that were at the time, deemed counter cultural, and still are to this day. The disciples, along with other spectators eagerly listened as Jesus rightly disturbed their instilled worldview in giving them the true meaning of "blessing" while also revealing that no one was qualified to fulfill the heart behind the law in its entirety, except Jesus.

    After explaining to the crowd how anger for one's brother is considered murder (even at the heart level) Jesus continues to ruffle feathers when embarking upon the topic of lust. He goes on to say that looking at a woman lustfully is equivalent to committing adultery. We may not fully understand the gravity of this statement considering adultery doesn't always have heavy implications in our present day culture. However, Jesus' audience, being well acquainted with the Law of Moses, knew exactly how provocative Jesus' statement actually was. The law clearly indicates that, "If a man commits adultery with another man's wife—with the wife of his neighbor—both the adulterer and the adulteress are to be put to death " (Leviticus 20:10, NIV). Jesus is saying that desiring a man or woman who does not belong to you and wanting him or her for yourself in your mind, is just as heinous as lying down with that person and committing the actual act—both predicaments deserve death. In saying this, Jesus unapologetically calls out every guilty listener by showcasing the sinful condition of their hearts while also illuminating the righteous, uncompromising standard of God. This truth especially called out the Pharisees, who, like whitewashed tombs were often presentable and "righteous" on the outside, but were merely corpses on the inside (Matthew 23:27-28).

  To put it blatantly, Jesus Himself defines lust as adultery and the punishment for adultery is death. Only Christ Himself was capable of living a perfectly righteous life as God in the flesh and saving sinners from such a grim reality.

Understanding God's Purposes for Sex

  I once asked the question, "Can a wife lust after her own husband?" Clearly, I didn't understand how that statement could be problematic. Typically, the word "lust" is used in reference to a strong desire that isn't godly. Having a strong longing or desire for one's spouse within the confines of marriage (in a manner that is loving, mutually edifying, and absent of idolatry) is *good*. By asking this question, I had mistakenly associated sinful lusts (something that is innately bad) with the marriage covenant as God intended it to be (something that is innately God-glorifying). Now, I'm not negating the fact that lust can still exist in a marriage. Perverted desires of the heart don't dissipate after vows are exchanged—whether that involves lusting after another person that isn't one's spouse, involving oneself in pornographic acts, abusing one's spouse to satisfy a selfish desire, etc., lust isn't just a single person's battle. However, in a marriage designed how God intended it to function (without perversion), sex is a worshipful transaction between husband and wife that paints a small portrait of God's passionate love for His very own bride.

God is not anti-sex as many Christians have unintentionally alluded in the church. He created it for His glory and has wired us accordingly. Surely, sex is a means of procreation (Genesis 1:28), but if that was its only purpose—well, He wouldn't have made it pleasurable. Within the marriage covenant, sex reiterates the oneness of the husband and wife that God has established to mirror the intimacy and oneness of Christ and His church brought forth through the gospel.

Instead of submitting to God's holy parameters as it relates to sex, we have defied them in ways unimaginable. In making God out to be a cosmic bully, merely existing to "keep us from having fun," we neglect to consider that perhaps, He knows what He's talking about. "For the Lord gives wisdom; from his mouth come knowledge and understanding" (Proverbs 2:6, NIV).

Our lust comes into the picture when we want what we want because we want it, all the while disregarding God's "wants." By lusting, we willingly entertain sexual longings and desires for individuals who do not belong to us. In doing so, we turn our backs on God's original purposes for sex in order to gratify our sinful desires. Our lustful mindsets deceive us into thinking that godly love and marital commitment are foolish, antiquated ideas—ultimately making lustful appetites appear to be logical, rationalized realities. This is not the case. God's will, will always and forever be *good, pleasing and perfect* (Romans 12:2).

Why Good Girls Fall Victim to Lust

For years, I welcomed lust with opened arms. I didn't filter what I saw on television, the movies I watched, or the music I listened to. Visualizing in my head what I often saw within those mediums fed my growing curiosity. The imagination is a powerful thing. Certainly, it's a gift from God, but sin can quickly taint that gift—providing ammunition for growing sexual curiosities. In my case, imaginative daydreaming quickly turned into actual dreaming, which eventually manifested into action.

Lust typically wins in the hearts of those who aren't completely won over by Christ. Not to say zealous Christians don't also struggle with lust, it's just easier to fall into the temptation if you were never grounded in the first place. If your main objective is to gratify yourself, of course, God's opinion on the matter of lust is irrelevant. But if your main objective is to please God through holiness, you're more inclined to not only take heed to what He says—but to obey as well, knowing that His ways supersede your momentary desires. In my case, I wanted to "do me" and let God cosign on it. Thus, I was more concerned about pleasing myself, all the while putting on the façade of appearing "good" instead of actually being "good" (in Christ).

My Struggle with Lust

"Let no one say when he is tempted, "I am being tempted by God"; for God cannot be tempted by evil, and He Himself does not tempt anyone. But each one is tempted when he is carried away and enticed by his own lust. Then when lust has conceived, it gives birth to sin; and when sin is accomplished, it brings forth death."
(James 1:13-15, NASB)

But each one is tempted when he is carried away and enticed by his own lust...

I can't remember a specific moment—a particular instance when I started feeling lustful. It sort of happened over time. I started having dreams in middle school of me simulating sexual acts. Though I didn't know what sex looked like or felt like, the shows I watched on television were enough to stimulate the sin inside of me. What is so crazy to me is that I was never introduced to sex or perverted things in my household. My parents didn't allow us to have cable because of the ridiculous stuff on TV. Thank the Lord, I was never sexually abused or molested, so I really had no reason for having that kind of lust in my heart when I was in essence sheltered. It's humbling to realize that *nobody had to teach me how to sin, it came innately*. Sure, the explicit content presented in the music I listened to didn't help the situation, but it just watered the seed that was already planted in my heart.

I got my first boyfriend at fifteen. It almost felt like redemption time. All of my life I felt like guys never liked me. I was the nerdy, awkward, black girl. It seemed like as soon as I got my eyebrows arched and started wearing my hair down, they took notice. Girls had been "dating" ever since middle school. Why had I been left out? Someone had finally shown interest in me, and I wasn't passing the opportunity by. After we started "going with each other," (which ultimately meant holding hands in the hallway and changing our relationship statuses on Facebook), I started dwelling on receiving my first kiss. Would it be epic like the movies? How would I feel? Who would initiate? Would it be awkward? Neither of us had kissed anyone before, so I had no idea what to expect. I began watching YouTube videos in the confines of my house, attempting to unleash the mystery behind kissing (as if it were rocket science). Surprisingly, it was never my desire to "kiss" (as in peck)—I instantly searched for videos of people making out. Being on my desktop computer at home searching for this stuff wasn't the wisest idea, but I was sure to delete the history after I was done. In retrospect, I had no concern about what God thought. I knew He saw me but did I care enough to stop? No. I had more fear inside me for my parents. If they found out—who knows what would have happened.

Ironically enough, I don't remember my first kiss. It was all a blur. I remember it was awkward, and I was kind of aggressive, but that's it. That kiss eventually led to a series of kisses and that was the highlight of our relationship. It's what I most looked forward to. Fast forward a couple of "sessions" later, and we were, of course, kissing right in front of my Algebra II class. That time is infused in my memory because it was one of the first times I felt something. It was the first time my flesh had actually responded to what was happening. I figured, we must have been doing something right, or had at least been getting better at it. I remember being on a little high after. What I didn't realize was that it would initiate a craving inside of me for more kisses, for an accelerated type of feeling. My feelings began to dictate me. None of the other kisses ever amounted to that one. I was disappointed. Why? Because contrary to the expectation I had in my mind, the other kisses didn't satisfy. I always wanted to advance and appease my growing curiosity. I eventually broke up with that boyfriend sometime after.

Then when lust has conceived, it gives birth to sin...

A year or so later I was sixteen and going about my business as a high school junior. Then enters boyfriend number two; we had been introduced to each other by a mutual friend, at church (of all places). Upon meeting him for the first time, there was no doubt in my mind that he was attractive. He was 5'10—not too tall, not too short. He was athletic, in shape and of the most radiant chocolate complexion. He asked for my number, and I felt like I would have been doing myself a disservice by *not* giving it to him. He called me a couple of hours after church that Sunday and it was a wrap from there. We started talking religiously. As we got to know one another, he eventually asked me to be his girlfriend a month or so later—and of course, I accepted. It couldn't have been fifteen minutes after we hung up the phone before I announced my relationship status on Facebook while simultaneously calling my girlfriends to unveil the news. I was beyond excited at that point—excitedly lame in retrospect, but nevertheless, excited. It was like a dream come true or something (in my sixteen-year-old mind). Attraction and relationship status aside, I do believe we had established grounds for a friendship during that month of "talking" which allowed me to be myself around him. I seriously started thinking, "hey this is someone I could marry." On top of all of that, he was "saved" too, which meant that he would wait until marriage to have sex with me (because that's where my head was at apparently). Because of all of these emotions (and hormones), I think I began to mentally see myself as his wife after some time had passed by—without the sex, of course. I started to open up to him, mentally and emotionally. He was the first boyfriend I had bothered to introduce to my dad! I had actually let this young man in my space. As I began to share my world with him, affection naturally came along with the territory.

  I knew he wasn't a virgin and likewise, he was aware of my stance for abstinence. He respected that. I can honestly say that he never did anything that I didn't allow. Which is scary because looking back—I allowed a lot, ultimately permitting my lust to advance. We made out, which was expected, considering my history in relationship number one. This time, I had accelerated my curiosity further by allowing him to touch me when kissing. I won't get explicit on that one—I'm sure you get the picture. It was something I often cherished and dreaded equally. Cherished in that it felt good, obviously, and dreaded because he was big on PDA and I wasn't about that life. I would have much rather done it in the privacy of my home when my parents weren't around in *secret*. Though I wasn't aware of it at the time, that's how I now know it was wrong. I was too ashamed to even tell my parents, it obviously wasn't acceptable behavior. Meaning—if in my mind it was knowingly unacceptable to my Christian parents, it couldn't have been pleasing to God either. It's amazing to me that even when I was doing my own thing, God still intentionally postured my parents as my covering to invoke a fear inside of me, which ultimately kept me from doing what I actually desired. Had my parents allowed me to be a wild child without any rules or structure, I wouldn't have seen my behavior as ill suited. I wasn't having sex, so my lusts were warranted in my mind. Like so many young girls, I was confusing my raging lusts for love. After all, that's what we see in the movies. It's what we read in Nicholas Sparks novels. Affection is just a reaction to love. I get it, and it's not completely false. What the world doesn't understand, however, is that it cannot merely react to something it is oblivious to. Love is a foreign concept to the world because it doesn't know Jesus. He's authentic love (1 John 3:16). What society operates in is lust—a counterfeit imitation of love. I didn't understand the difference.

Our relationship lasted about three months, though it felt like we had been together for ages because I had invested so much energy into the relationship. He broke up with me before he went off to college because of the distance. Though we had formally broken up, and I was heartbroken about it, I still had emotional ties with him. We would still chat from time to time. I began to live in a fantasyland of what "could be." I actually started to make logic out of it; the only reason why he broke it off with me in the first place was because he went to college. So in my mind, I started to plan my future life with him. College was a year out for me, so if I somehow went to a school somewhere near his vicinity, we would then have a license to be together. It made perfect sense. Later, I soon realized that he had been talking to another girl who resided in a location that was further away from him than I was. Truth being, he just wasn't that into me anymore. God was telling me through that situation that I didn't need to be with him. He had closed the door that I had voluntarily opened. In refusing to let go by remaining emotionally invested in him for nearly a year post our break up, I willingly invited preventable hurt into my heart.

It took me a while to get over that relationship for some reason. I recall feeling defeated and hopeless for a short period. All of the time. All of the emotion. Wasted. I felt less than good enough. A car ride with my sister put things into perspective. I don't remember what compelled her to say this, but she basically told me (in a vexed tone might I add—clearly she was over my nonsense) that this man was not my life, and I should stop wallowing in my sorrows as if he were. That hit me deep. I had made an idol out of him. All of the time. All of the emotion— had been poured out on him instead of God. That was precisely why the pain cut me so profoundly. Not only did I idolize him, but as soon as he left, withdrawal hit. I developed an emotional lust for him. I wanted to hear his voice, know how he was doing, and even stalk him on social media. I believe God strategically snatched him away from me to reveal to me the depths of my own heart.

...and when sin is accomplished, it brings forth death...

I stopped dating after that. Some say I was bitter (which might have been a slightly valid claim), but honestly, I just had a lot going on. My high school graduation was approaching, I was on my way to college, and a new season of life had officially commenced. Though I had entertained someone during this transitional period, nobody ever reclaimed that "boyfriend" title again—until my sophomore year of college.

At first, I had no intention of entertaining my third boyfriend. He went against every preference known to me. Even so, I grew fond of him. I'm realizing that this fondness was an acquirement that developed as a result of his initial admiration of me. Had he never taken an interest in me in the first place, I don't know if I would have paid attention to him in that way. Whether that is good or bad, I nevertheless developed a genuine liking for him. Though he had a plethora of personality traits that intrigued me (a funny personality, light-heartedness, authenticity, ambition etc.) other characteristics dissatisfied me (vulgarity, lack of filter, etc.). Knowing all of this from the beginning, I consciously made a decision to get into the relationship anyway. I chose to overlook the negatives for the sake of potential (a mistake so many of us ladies make in hopes that we can somehow "change" a man in the process of dating him). From the beginning, I was aware that this relationship wasn't something God approved of. I remember praying to God, asking Him if the relationship was something I should involve myself in. Yet, even when He answered, I stopped listening and ignored many signs sent as warnings. I knew in my heart of hearts that at the time, he wasn't able to lead me towards the things of Christ, but I didn't care enough to submit to God at that point. I much preferred my plan over God's will because I was tired of waiting. Having no real example of young, black, godly relationships in my life convinced me that they didn't exist. I didn't have enough faith in God to trust that He had something better out there for me. Rather, I trusted in what was available and clearly seen.

Our relationship accelerated from that point forward. This territory outside of God's will was scary business, but I dove in head on. My lust issues had never been officially addressed, so my desires advanced exponentially during the course of this relationship. Being that I was still in school in Tampa while he resided in Jacksonville, long distance played a significant role as well, which didn't help the situation. So when we did see each other, it was intense.

Without getting too graphic, we were affectionately involved in every way possible without having actual intercourse. It's definitely a period I'm not proud of, but it happened. The lust of my flesh was something that had become so full blown and innate to my body that I was accustomed to it at that point. Though I enjoyed the physical gratification of pleasing my flesh, the spiritual ramifications of my behavior were overwhelming. I literally felt at war with the Holy Spirit — which makes perfect sense since the Spirit of God will always be directly opposed to the works of the flesh (Galatians 5:17). I had never experienced conviction so severely before. Peace had left me, and either way I felt like I was losing. In my flesh, I was never truly satisfied, and in my spirit, I was betraying God. My heart condemned me. What's funny about the situation is that I was so focused on not having sexual intercourse when all along God wasn't concerned about my technicalities. He had never been. He was looking at my heart—the source of it all. Did I really think that allowing this boyfriend to do everything to me, except penetrate, actually glorified God or pleased Him in any way? In no way, but somehow, I tried to make sense of it all. I now realize that the Holy Spirit was convicting me to save me from myself. He had convicted me to protect me. It's not that He didn't want me to have fun—it's that He loved me too much to let me continue to thrive in the deadly place I willingly interjected myself into (Hebrews 12:6). Most of all, He was drawing me back to Him. Even in my sin, His mercy and grace kept me from a host of evil things I had ignorantly exposed myself to. This was the point in my life when I realized, I couldn't have my cake and eat it too. Following Jesus for real required sacrifice on my part. I had to make a crucial decision. Continue to wallow in my lust addiction and thrive there, or surrender my heart to God without compromise. Praise God I chose the latter.

What was so liberating about the entire process was that Jesus really reassured me that He was better than what I was leaving behind. However, that reassurance would have aborted itself had I never stepped out on faith in the first place. Though my flesh felt like it was going through some serious symptoms of withdrawal, moving forward was beyond worth it. I could never have imagined that it was possible to thrive in Christ alone. In my former way of thinking, young people who "only had Jesus" only said that because they couldn't get a man—as if having a man were the epitome of life. But even after having had a man, I'm a living witness that God is legitimately better. I wish I had more eloquent words, but it's as simple as that. A man can only do so much—and even at his best, he's incapable of filling your every need and desire. God has graced me to realize that everything I've ever wanted in life is wrapped up in Him: intimacy, salvation, acceptance, love, peace, joy, security, faithfulness, guidance, confidence, self-esteem, value, forgiveness, grace, redemption, purity, healing, beauty, inheritance...the list is endless. I had to stop deeming Jesus as some alternative option when all along He was fighting to be my everything.

Temptation

I can't lie and say that temptation doesn't still exist. The temptation to feed my lust can sometimes still be a very real thing. Sometimes, it only takes an unexpected movie scene. Other times a familiar fragrance. I can't help that those things exist outside of my control, but I can choose not to dwell on the memories that they may initiate (Philippians 4:8). I can choose to starve my flesh and make it my slave (1 Corinthians 9:27). I can choose to renew my mind and combat thoughts that are displeasing to God (Romans 12:2). I can choose not to stalk my exes on social media. Sometimes, we go digging things up knowing good and well that they're bound to stir up sinful affections within us that ought not to be revived. I know a lot of times, I deem myself less sensitive than I actually am. Resistance becomes that much harder when I start flirting with the very thing I'm supposed to be fighting. I know a lot of times when I'm tempted to engross my mind in the memories of "what used to be," I tend to only think about what made my flesh feel good at the time. I never seem to remember the heartache, guilt, shame, borderline depression, anxiety, and sorrow it caused me in the long run. And let's not forget all that Christ endured on the cross for that very sin. He didn't die for our lusts just for us to go back and lay in them again (2 Peter 2:22). That's exactly the enemy's scheme. We must outwit his played out arrangements.

The only difference between my temptation now, versus my temptation in these recollections is that back then I tried to resist in my own strength—now I rely on the Holy Spirit's power. Just like I needed God to save me then, I still need God to sanctify and keep me throughout this journey. We must remain encouraged and focused on Christ, not on our own propensity to sin when faced with temptations such as lust. "Because He Himself suffered when He was tempted, He is able to help those who are being tempted" (Hebrews 2:18, NIV).

Though Jesus is our advocate, we also have a conscious part to play in all of this. Romans 8:13 tells us, "For if you live according to the flesh, you will die; but if by the Spirit you put to death the misdeeds of the body, you will live" (NIV). God has given us incredible insight into His Will through His Word. Keeping this in mind, Scripture tells us in advance that **by** the Holy Spirit, **we** are empowered to put to death the misdeeds of our bodies. The Holy Spirit enables us to put our sin to death, but it's up to us at the end of the day to make that conscious effort. Knowing this, why would we intentionally succumb ourselves to tempting people, places, things, and atmospheres—knowing good and well that after it's all said and done, our flesh gets more of a win out of those encounters than our spirit? If our goal is to mature in Christ, how can we even attempt to do so by willingly placing ourselves in environments that are conducive to sin? Putting to death the misdeeds of the body is a big deal, and surely not easy by any means. However, it is beyond worth it, for only the children of God have the honor of being led by the Spirit of God (Romans 8:14).

All of Me

Have you ever heard the song, "All of Me" [1] by John Legend? It's quite refreshing if I say so myself. Though the verses of this song compel me to believe that Legend was inspired by a woman, most likely his wife, for some reason, the chorus always reminds me of the gospel. "You're my end and my beginning, even when I lose I'm winning. 'Cause I give you allll of me...and you give me allll of you." It's such a beautiful exchange—God, the Alpha and Omega, the Beginning and the End, the First and the Last (Revelation 22:13) *willingly* gave all of Himself to us. Though sin made it appear as if we were losing, and death threatened to overtake us, Jesus faithfully won the battle over sin and death—making us winners in Him.

You might be thinking, I'm being one of those deep fried super saved Christians... I'm really not though, I promise. Jesus Himself told the Sadducees and Pharisees that the greatest commandment in the Law is to "Love the Lord your God with all your heart and with all your soul and with all your mind" (Matthew 22:37, NIV). Though it sounds inviting and rather effortless to love a holy, compassionate, merciful and flawless God—it's one thing to love Him with our lip service and another to love Him with *all of us*. Understanding the depth of this scripture is especially imperative when battling sins such as lust. How can we claim to love God with all that we are when He's constantly competing against our lustful affections?

Before even attempting to love God with all of ourselves, we must first recognize His identity. "The Lord, your God" is what the Scripture says. He is the only One we ought to love in this capacity, less a person or thing "lords" over our lives in the place of *the* Lord. The Greek word used here for "the Lord" is *kyrios*. It refers to "he to whom a person or thing belongs, about which he has power of deciding; master, lord." It also refers to "God, the Messiah," which is how it's being used in this particular context. I find it interesting that servants used this word to greet their earthly masters. They understood to whom they belonged and acted accordingly. How much more should believers do the same for the Supreme Master—Jesus Christ? (Philippians 2:10-11)

Loving God properly also requires that we understand our association with Him. To the believer, He is *your* God. The Law could have very well said *the* God, but it instead makes it personal to us. Though it can appear intimidating to love a supreme, omnipotent God as flawed beings, it is comforting to know that through Christ, He is *our* God. Just as the Jews were God's people in the former covenant, Christ's followers have this same sense of belonging under the new covenant.

Jesus speaks of three ways to love the Lord, your God in the book of Matthew: "with all your heart, with all your soul, and with all your mind." Loving God with every fiber of our being enables us to replace ungodly and potentially lustful desires with a Spirit-led, godly appetite. In doing so, we embark on a lifelong journey of learning how to love God holistically as He instructs.

I.   With All Your Heart

This can be scary. Especially considering that many of us attempt to love God with the same hearts that have lusted after something at some point in time. After all, Scripture does say that "The heart is deceitful above all things, and desperately sick; who can understand it?" (Jeremiah 17:9, ESV). While yes, it may appear a bit intimidating at first— Christ allows us to freely love God because He has wiped our consciences clean of the guilt caused by sin, including lust (Hebrews 9:14).

Kardia is the Greek noun used In Matthew 22 for "heart." It literally means "the soul or mind, as it is the fountain and seat of the thoughts, passions, desires, appetites, affections, purposes, endeavors." The heart is the "central, inmost part of anything." Our minds hold more power than we give it credit for. These minds of ours can literally influence the throne of our hearts by simply doing what they do best, *thinking*. What do you think about? Better yet, what do you watch and listen to? Is it good? Is it true? Is it noble? Is it pure? Is it lovely? Is it admirable? Is it excellent? Is it praiseworthy, as Philippians 4:8 encourages? If not, we give license for our hearts to desire appetites, affections, purposes, endeavors, and passions other than God. In doing so, we refrain from loving God with all of ourselves.

II.   With All Your Soul

The Greek word for "soul," *psyche*, has a similar meaning as *kardia*. Though it is also "the seat of the feelings desires, affections and aversions," *psyche* is distinct in that it is used to describe our "moral being designed for everlasting life." This soul can experience everlasting life with or without God because of sin. Whether we choose God or not—our souls were wired for forever. On Earth, we can either feed our souls with the Spirit of God and birth life eternally or feed our souls with our flesh causing eternal death (Romans 8:13). By submitting to what the flesh may desire in a particular moment, we give death a fighting chance at giving us life. By taking this route, we will consequently become disappointed by the deceitfulness of sin every time we choose it over God. By submitting to what the Holy Spirit desires instead, though conflict may still arise internally, we elect for true life instead of death.

III.   With All Your Mind

"Mind" in Matthew 22:37 comes from the Greek word *dilanoia*. It is "the faculty of understanding, feeling and desiring." Personally, loving God with my feelings and desires has always been most challenging for me. I'm like, "God, do you *really* want me to love you with all of my mind, because it's pretty messed up." Of course, He's well-versed with the complexities of my mind, but even so, it's a scary thought to know that God almighty knows my heart—the good, bad, and the dirty. After all, I tend to take comfort in the fact that people aren't mind readers. It's entirely too easy to say one thing to someone while thinking another. Since it's so incredibly effortless to outwit people, I am sometimes tempted to use this same approach with God. Yet, this temptation is quickly dismissed as I'm always reminded that God already knows the things I successfully hide from people. He knows, and He hasn't left yet, nor will He.

As an introvert, most thoughts typically stay in my mind without ever manifesting into action. Consequently, I usually have a lot of mental activity going on at all times. Due to the fact that this is how I operate, I have to be especially intentional about surrendering my mind to God. As it relates to lust, I have come to terms with the fact that I can't watch everything. As a visual person, I can't watch certain movies or shows without my curiosities and thoughts veering left. Something may start off as innocent, but my mind will dwell on it and take it to another level without me even realizing. Thus, in knowing myself and how my mind operates, I have to be especially careful to download "God-glorifying" things into my mind and heart.

I have noticed that we as women think completely differently than men. Though this seems like a "duh" statement, it's so true. Take getting to know someone, for example, some men are simple—they may talk to you, they may even have hidden motives to pursue you, however in the beginning stages, they're most likely just trying to get a feel for who you are. Women, on the other hand, operate completely differently. At the same stage in a relationship, I have been notorious for having already married, birthed a couple of kids, and will currently be in the process of growing old with someone in my head before our first date even commences. We are very imaginative and introspective, to say the least.

Because I'm so imaginative, loving God with my heart can be challenging, however, it's most rewarding for me when I'm intentional about doing so, because the heart is the wellspring of life (Psalm 4:23). Sometimes, I think about how much more effective and God-glorifying it would be if I simply redirected the energy I sometimes store up dwelling on fleshly desires and exerted that same mind power on the Lord by meditating on His Word. Using the imagination to glorify God is so incredibly satisfying—even worshipful. My desire is for the Lord to constantly redeem my thoughts in such a way that former sinful thoughts become adoring praises overflowing out of my mind, onto my lips, unto God (Psalm 34:1).

Exhortation

I wrote this chapter not to boast in my sins, but rather to boast in God's grace that has faithfully covered me throughout my entire journey—especially as it relates to lust. God is not a respecter of persons (Romans 2:11). He is not a God who would deliver me and leave you by the wayside. God is able to redeem your life of sin for His glory. He is able to remove the stain of guilt that sin inevitably brands on your conscience by cleansing it with His blood (Hebrews 9:14). He is able to heal the deepest incisions in your soul that have been invaded by the deceitfulness of sin. He is able, He wants to heal you, and He will—if you let Him. Regardless of the sexual sin at hand (pornography, masturbation, fornication, etc), regardless of how many times you have committed that same sin over and over again, you aren't beyond grace's headquarters. Your story doesn't have to sound like mine. What links the testimony of a believer with another believer isn't the individual experience, but the overarching power of Christ to save regardless of the circumstances. Be encouraged.

IDLENESS

"For we are his workmanship, created in Christ Jesus for good works, which God prepared beforehand, that we should walk in them." (Ephesians 2:10, ESV)

Recently, I was watching this documentary on the National Geographic channel called *Prison Nation*.[1] Its main focus was prison systems in America and how the institution isn't doing an optimal job reinstating inmates into society. Not only that, but American prisons have reached full capacity in many cities, formulating an overcrowding issue. They decided to drive the concern close to home by introducing an inmate by the name of Chris Brown (not the celebrity) to the audience. Brown was sent to Salinas Valley State Prison in California after committing an alleged robbery. What was most heartbreaking to me wasn't the fact that Brown was sent to prison in the first place, but the fact that he didn't even receive a jail cell upon arrival. Due to the population congestion, prisoners were sent to an on-site gym, where they basically were "warehoused." There weren't enough cells to house everyone so inmates were forced to sleep on bunk beds three levels high with their peers as roommates. As a result, many fights broke out and this type of hostile environment created many challenges when trying to maintain safety.

What I found even more unfortunate and brings me to the topic of this chapter, is how idle these men had become—mainly for reasons outside of their control. There were no recreational activities for them. No work to be done. Literally, most of them lay around in their beds all day thirsty for something, anything to do. Typically, violence happened more frequently because...what else was there to do? What toil that can take on one's mentality, to feel purposeless—merely existing to die. Unfortunately, this is a reality not just for these inmates at Salinas Valley State Prison, but for everyday people like you and me.

What Does it Mean to be Idle, & Why is it a Sin?

When attempting to determine the initial meaning behind a particular word in the Bible, I always find it useful to look up the original Greek/Hebrew word used in its proper context within Scripture. We try to translate words into English as best as we can, but oftentimes, there are different implications for those words in present day culture. Not only that, but the English language doesn't even house all of the words, phrases, and intricacies provided by the original language. I always find it helpful to read multiple versions of a verse in addition to looking up the original Greek/Hebrew word intended for a Scripture or term I'm having a difficult time grasping. I say all of that because I am a huge advocate for personal study. Outside of reading this book, I want you to be able to interpret Scripture (for what it's actually saying) for yourself.

I never really thought of idleness as a sin until recently. Therefore, I had to ask myself—what is sin? It may seem like a basic question, but really what is sin? If I asked you that question, would you be able to provide a clear, definitive answer?

Sin comes from the root word *chata* which means to literally miss the way (mark), go wrong, incur guilt or condemnation, etc. What way or mark is the Bible referring to, and how do we know if we miss it? God sets this mark or standard. Because God is righteous, His standard is none other than perfection. God unveils this standard to humanity through the law of Moses (first five books of the Bible). The only person in all of human history, who was ever able to fulfill this law by keeping all of its commandments, was in fact Jesus—God in the flesh (John 1). He lived a sinless life. In Romans 3, Paul is very clear when he says that everyone misses the mark and falls short of the glory of God except Christ, which is why faith in Him is the only way to be justified. Thus, in order for me to determine if idleness is a sin, I had to first ask myself—was Jesus ever idle?

We could intensely study the New Testament to answer that question, but it's likely that you would stop reading this book. I'll leave that for your own personal study. Instead, if I look up the definition of the word "idle" I'm confident that the answer to the question will be just as obvious. Idle comes from the Greek word *argos*, which means to be free from labor; at leisure. The second definition of the word idle means to be lazy, shunning the labor which one ought to perform. To answer the original question, was Jesus ever lazy, shunning the labor he was sent to perform? Absolutely not! Why? Because everything Jesus did in the gospels came from a place of purpose. God is not a God of chance or coincidence. He is a God of purpose and intentionality. Jesus did everything His Father did/instructed because He and the Father are one (John 10:30). So, why did Jesus come in the first place? He came to save us from our sins, simply put (1 Timothy 1:15). In doing this He fulfilled the Law and prophecies, did the will of His Father, healed the sick, opened the eyes of the blind, fed thousands, walked on water and died on a cross. However, he never did *anything* outside of this purpose to provide eternal life through salvation for sinners like you and I. Even as Jesus worked as a carpenter, as menial as it may sound, His Father was still glorified in that season of His life. As a carpenter, Jesus was able to relate to us. After all, living a life as a carpenter filled with seemingly trivial day-to-day responsibilities doesn't appear all that glamorous at first glance. However, God made it so that our High Priest and King wouldn't be far removed from us and could ultimately relate. Do you think that happened by accident? Everything that Jesus did was on purpose and for His Father's glory (John 8:54). In determining if idleness is a sin, I also have to consult other scriptures to further prove the legitimacy of my claim.

The book of Proverbs announces more blatantly how idleness is displeasing to God:

- "The soul of the sluggard craves and gets nothing, while the soul of the diligent is richly supplied" (Proverbs 13:4, ESV).
- "Whoever is slack in his work is a brother to him who destroys" (Proverbs 18:9, ESV).
- "Slothfulness casts into a deep sleep, and an idle person will suffer hunger" (Proverbs 19:15, ESV).

If you think that's not relevant because those scriptures are from the Old Testament, here are New Testament scriptures:

- "...If anyone is not willing to work, let him not eat. For we hear that some among you walk in idleness, not busy at work, but busybodies" (2 Thessalonians 3:10b-11, ESV).
- "We do not want you to become lazy, but to imitate those who through faith and patience inherit what has been promised" (Hebrews 6:12, NIV).

Idleness can be an Identity Issue

Referencing everything from the above section, I had to ask myself—why do we as humans become idle in the first place? I think a lot of it has to do with identity. When you know whose you are, it's easier to determine what it is you're supposed to be doing here on Earth. Even animals serve individual, distinct purposes within their lifetimes. Take the Pacific salmon for example. One of its sole purposes is to reproduce! In fact, after spawning, most species of these salmon die soon after. Or better yet, the cockroach! Have you ever wondered why they exist as you frantically rummaged to kill one? Besides adhering to its repulsive, filthy nature, roaches also trap nitrogen in their systems as they feed on decaying organic matter. When they eventually dispel of their fecal waste, nitrogen is released simultaneously—providing nourishment for the soil. Even weeds serve a purpose in the grand scheme of things by shielding the ground from water and wind erosion. If all of creation is intelligently wired as to fulfill these practical purposes in life, are we as humans any less purposeful? Are we not worth more as image bearers of God? Though we actually carry a weightier purpose than all of these examples combined, we ironically live in such a way that is more purposefully impoverished than the life of a mere animal. I wonder how that makes our heavenly Father feel?

    In understanding how and why mere animals function to better the entire ecosystem, it's also even more vital that Christians realize how they ought to function to better the kingdom of God. While writing this chapter, I thought I knew for sure that a Christian's purpose is to make disciples and fulfill the Great Commission! But then, I thought that even though that may be accurate, this command Jesus gives isn't our full overarching purpose, rather, it's a byproduct of something greater. I believe Paul gives a pretty substantial description of humanity's purpose in Colossians 1:16; "For in him all things were created: things in heaven and on earth, visible and invisible, whether thrones or powers or rulers or authorities; all things have been created through him and for him" (NIV). We were created for Jesus. That sounds like a blanket statement if you ask me. We were created for the glory of Jesus, we were created for the pleasure of Jesus, we were created to spread the work of Jesus, we were created to worship Jesus, we were created to be the bride of Jesus, we were created to enjoy Jesus...and so on and so forth. This purpose is so consistent with the creation account as well, showing the validity of God's Word. Genesis 1:26 says, "Then God said, 'Let us make mankind in our image, in our likeness, so that they may rule over the fish in the sea and the birds in the sky, over the livestock and all the wild animals, and over all the creatures that move along the ground'" (NIV). Even from the beginning, God crafted man by Himself for Himself. Why else would He make man in His image and give him permission to rule? To showcase His glory, that's why. After Adam sinned, however, it all went downhill from there. Humans could no longer fully experience God because we had missed the mark. Man's world had been shaken and shattered. God's original purposes for us were tainted by sin. Jesus had to come back to reconcile us back to the Father and pay the price for our sins in order to reinstate godly purpose in our lives.

How unfortunate it is to know this purpose and still be idle. I can honestly say that my excuse isn't that I remain ignorant to this purpose; my excuse is that I'd rather ignore/reject it. Though I was made for God by God, sometimes I act as if that isn't good enough. That's why at times, I sleep my problems away or spend my days doing worthless menial things instead of praying. What really kills me about myself is that at times, I feel as if I have "arrived" with Jesus. Of course, this is a lie from the pit of hell, but it becomes a reality in my head at times, which ultimately makes me place limits on God. In my mind sometimes, I'm like "this is as good as it's going to get so why press harder in seeking Christ, what's the point?" So, I stop praying consistently. I lose my motivation to worship. I take my days for granted. Meanwhile, souls are perishing and I'm just too consumed in my own idleness and disobedience to notice or care.

Sometimes, the opposite holds true. I find myself "doing" a whole lot of the *wrong* things—just for the sake of doing something. My actions at times lack both purpose and focus. I'm the type of person who doesn't like to sit still. So, when I feel as if I should be up to something, there's no stopping me. I'm like "Jesus, You're taking too long, I need something to do!" So I get invested in a whole bunch of different ministries, activities, pastimes etc. Meanwhile, I can imagine Jesus saying, "But I already told you what to do, you just don't trust me enough to be obedient."

I consider this, "I'm going to do everything else except what I'm supposed to do" attitude to be a form of idleness as well (2 Thessalonians 3:11). I must admit, one of my biggest distractions these days is social media. Scrolling down my news feed and being enticed by pictures and statuses can keep me occupied for hours at a time. Clearly, this isn't conducive to my overall productivity, but sometimes that's honestly all I want to do. By being purely lazy, I can procrastinate to do the work I ought to be doing and complain about my ungodly to-do-list after the fact. Being this way, my lack of discipline doesn't serve God's purposes—I'm either a.) too lazy or b.) too busy, to fulfill them.

Biblical Examples of Idleness

"Then Jesus went with them to a place called Gethsemane, and he said to his disciples, 'Sit here, while I go over there and pray.' And taking with him Peter and the two sons of Zebedee, he began to be sorrowful and troubled. Then he said to them, 'My soul is very sorrowful, even to death; remain here, and watch with me.' And going a little farther he fell on his face and prayed, saying, 'My Father, if it be possible, let this cup pass from me; nevertheless, not as I will, but as you will.' And he came to the disciples and found them sleeping. And he said to Peter. 'So, could you not watch with me one hour? Watch and pray that you may not enter into temptation. The spirit indeed is willing, but the flesh is weak.' Again, for the

second time, he went away and prayed, 'My Father, if this cannot pass unless I drink it, your will be done.' And again he came and found them sleeping, for their eyes were heavy. So, leaving them again, he went away and prayed for the third time, saying the same words again. Then he came to the disciples and said to them, 'Sleep and take your rest later on. See, the hour is at hand, and the Son of Man is betrayed into the hands of sinners. Rise, let us be going; see, my betrayer is at hand.'" (Matthew 26: 36-46 ESV)

This passage of scripture pretty much explains itself—especially as it pertains to idleness. But just so we're on the same page, I want to highlight Jesus' commands in this account:

"Sit here, while I go over there and pray."

I don't believe Jesus meant this literally. Don't shoot me for saying that. He didn't just want the disciples to merely sit there as He prayed, like children being dropped off at daycare. Instead, Jesus wanted the disciples to mirror His actions, like students shadowing their instructor. Jesus was praying, so He wanted His disciples to pray alongside Him, especially because this was right before His crucifixion. His second command clarifies this claim furthermore…

"My soul is very sorrowful, even to death; remain here, and watch with me."

Remain here, and watch with me—it supports the previous command. The first time Jesus wanted the disciples to pray, however, this time, He emphasized the need to watch *with* Him. What were the disciples watching for? The answer is embedded in Ephesians 6:12 "For our struggle is not against flesh and blood, but against the rulers, against the authorities, against the powers of this dark world and against the spiritual forces of evil in the heavenly realms" (NIV). The disciples weren't supposed to be watching for any physical attack. They were instead, supposed to be watching for the spiritual attacks approaching them. Temptation and betrayal were all crouching at their doors, just waiting to attack. "Watching" via prayer would have given the disciples the spiritual strength to endure the atrocious timeline ahead of them. Meanwhile, Jesus was sorrowful because the sin of the world was on His shoulders. His Father was about to forsake Him. He was about to endure excruciating physical and spiritual wrath for the sins of all—and He was well aware of it, after all, He is God. He submitted to His Father's will regardless of how He may have "felt" in that moment. But the disciples were far too concerned about the "now" of the things of this world to take Jesus' commands seriously. They responded with the following action:

"And he came to the disciples and found them sleeping."

What! Of all the things out there to do, they decided to sleep in this moment. I'm sure they had a long day but seriously—Jesus didn't ask for much. He was doing all of the work really. The disciples shunned the work they were to perform (watching and praying), in exchange for rest. Rest has its time and place—this was not one of them. Jesus then singled out Peter:

"And he said to Peter. 'So, could you not watch with me one hour? Watch and pray that you may not enter into temptation. The spirit indeed is willing, but the flesh is weak.'"

Not too long after this occurrence, Peter was tempted and he denied Christ three times! He was so consumed with the physical, that he lost sight of the spiritual. Before he denied Christ, Peter caught himself "fighting" for Jesus (as if Jesus was incapable of saving Himself) upon His arrest. "Simon Peter then, having a sword, drew it and struck the high priest's slave, and cut off his right ear; and the slave's name was Malchus. So Jesus said to Peter, 'Put the sword into the sheath; the cup which the Father has given Me, shall I not drink it?...'" (John 18:10-11, NASB). Peter was "gung ho" about fighting for Jesus physically, but what he didn't understand was that this earthly perspective was insignificant and irrelevant compared to what Jesus was about to do on the cross. Jesus even called Peter, Satan (Matthew 16:23) for having this mentality. Peter was a.) too lazy to pray for what mattered and b.) too busy fighting physical battles to understand the greater spiritual war at hand. God's purposes weren't being served through Peter at all at that point, showcasing Peter's idleness and oblivion simultaneously. Jesus then prayed again, providing a tangible example for the disciples to emulate.

"Again, for the second time, he went away and prayed, 'My Father, if this cannot pass unless I drink it, your will be done.'"

Jesus was referring to the cup of wrath He had to drink—the just wage for the sins of all humanity. The weight of sin was upon Him and He was feeling its effects. Jesus knew that He is the only way to salvation. Nobody comes to the Father except through Him. He was well aware of His purpose. That didn't make the burden any easier for Him. I believe this prayer exhibits Jesus' humanity at its best! No, Jesus wasn't trying to punk out of His assignment. Rather, this prayer illustrates just how sorrowful, and grieved He was—yet His committal to submission still shined through the unfathomable darkness He was experiencing. Feelings didn't dictate Jesus' actions, faithfulness did. The disciples didn't take heed to His example...

"And again he came and found them sleeping, for their eyes were heavy."

The struggle was real for the disciples at this point. Their eyes were heavy and everything. They were not being disobedient just for the sake of being disobedient. They were genuinely tired! How could they have been functional in the events to come if they weren't well rested?

"So, leaving them again, he went away and prayed for the third time, saying the same words again. Then he came to the disciples and said to them, 'Sleep and take your rest later on. See, the hour is at hand, and the Son of Man is betrayed into the hands of sinners. Rise, let us be going; see, my betrayer is at hand.'"

At that point, Jesus didn't even say anything to the disciples about "watching and praying." I can imagine that He was frustrated that they were consistently being idle and disobedient at such a time. He just went back and prayed again. After, He told the disciples that there would be a time when they could rest—that was not the time. The events preceding His crucifixion were about to commence, and the disciples were clearly ill-prepared for what was to come. They had no more time left to prepare; it was about to get real whether they were ready or not.

What the disciples deemed as innocent rest actually disadvantaged them in the long run. I'm sure they thought the sleep would help them function later. I'm sure they started praying and ended up drifting off soon thereafter. I'm sure they had every excuse in the book. But the end result was not only idleness but disobedience. They were not equipped for the events to come, as they were operating in their flesh.

I am similar to the disciples—maybe even worse. The same disdain I express in regard to their behavior, I have to mine. It's so easy to sleep a little here, eat a little there, talk on the phone, get on social media, etc. instead of keeping watch. I have personally felt God tugging on my heart for me to spend time in prayer, and I push it off until I do what I want to do first. Jesus sometimes takes a backseat to my priorities and that's not okay because He ought to be my only priority.

The Lord has placed an urgency on my heart to write this book because "good girls" are perishing everyday due to ignorance of the truth. Not only that, but Jesus is coming back for His bride very soon. Those who aren't in Christ will perish. Christians are not supposed to be surprised when this happens. Instead, we should be expectant. This expectancy should motivate us to win souls for Christ. 1 Thessalonians 5:6-8 says: "So then let us not sleep, as others do, but let us keep awake and be sober. For those who sleep, sleep at night, and those who get drunk, are drunk at night. But since we belong to the day, let us be sober, having put on the breastplate of faith and love, and for a helmet the hope of salvation" (ESV). Spiritual alertness is imperative. We cannot be asleep to our purposes, nor can we be asleep to the events to come. Just as Jesus dying on the cross was a definitive occurrence, cosigned by God Himself, the same holds true for Jesus' return. We have an event to prepare for, but are we ready? We can't be if idleness continually takes precedence over purpose in our lives.

Jesus Reigns Over EVERYTHING, including idleness...

I am both convicted and encouraged by the account of Jesus and the disciples at Gethsemane. Convicted by the fact that I am no better than the disciples (including Peter), and encouraged by the fact that Jesus still died on the cross in the very face of idleness, and all sin for that matter. Though the disciples allowed their flesh to get the best of them, refused to keep watch and remained blatantly disobedient—Jesus still laid down His life for them. What kind of person does that after such betrayal? Jesus does! I love how Paul said it, "Very rarely will anyone die for a righteous man, though for a good person someone might possibly dare to die. But God demonstrates his own love for us in this: While we were still sinners, Christ died for us" (Romans 5:7-8, NIV). If that's not hope, I don't know what is. Jesus' faithfulness dominates my sin. His grace crushes my inconsistencies, my laziness, my whatever—just fill in the blank. "But where sin increased, grace increased all the more" (Romans 5:20). Sin never overpowers grace! Regardless of how large, filthy, disgusting, evil, and unforgivable our sins may appear—they don't compare to the soul-saving, radical, powerful, life changing, righteous, all-consuming grace of Christ.

Action Isn't Necessarily the Remedy

When combating the sin of idleness, I'm often tempted to "do, do, do." It's intuitive to think that way. How do I stop being lazy? Get up and do something of course! It seems easy enough. However, I have to check myself when I am tempted to think this way. Yes, obedience is imperative and we all know that faith without works is dead (James 2:17). However, we cannot go through this life thinking that behavior modification will save us. Fighting idleness with action isn't always the solution. Don't get me wrong, discipline is in fact necessary when combating idleness, that goes without saying. What's more important in my opinion is that prior to acting in any capacity, we seek Jesus. The action *should* come after. It is imperative to ask the Lord for clarity concerning what we are to do and where we are to go in life. Whether it's something as minute as washing dishes or something as major as getting married—if we don't know the answer to something, searching the Scriptures and praying for wisdom is essential! We should not be content going through the motions as idle beings or doing work just for the sake of doing work. If we could save ourselves from idleness by merely doing better and trying harder, there would be no need for a Savior. Our own works just don't cut it in and of themselves, which is why in those difficult times of confusion when we are lacking clarity and direction, it only makes sense to seek the One who mapped out life from its conception. Ultimately, His purposes and plans prevail (Proverbs 19:21).

Don't Exactly Quit Your Day Job

When writing to the church at Thessalonica, Paul notes, "For you yourselves know how you ought to imitate us, because we were not idle when we were with you, nor did we eat anyone's bread without paying for it, but with toil and labor we worked night and day, that we might not be a burden to any of you" (2 Thessalonians 3:7-8, ESV). Paul still used 'tentmaking' to acquire income (Acts 18:3) as he was fulfilling his purposes by sharing the gospel. At first glance, tentmaking could be perceived as meaningless behavior. How is this act contributing to the larger calling over Paul's life? How is it glorifying God? Well, Paul didn't want to burden anyone. He used his skillset to gain income so that he could freely share the gospel without having to ask for compensation in return. He wasn't trying to "hustle" anyone into salvation. Now, that's not a criticism to full-time ministry. God very well purposes some to do just that. Paul also writes that those who preach the gospel should receive their living from the gospel (1 Corinthians 9:14). Though he had every right to receive compensation from people, he decided not to. This goes to show that just because you are working a day job, it doesn't mean you are a less competent Christian. You could very well be walking in purpose in using your job as a financial and social means of edifying the Kingdom. Even if you can't stand your job, your feeling doesn't necessarily mean that it's not a part of God's will for your life. Even the things that seem insignificant and purposeless to us as finite human beings could be the very things God uses for our good and His glory. Romans 8:28 reminds us that "...all things God works for the good of those who love him, who have been called according to his purpose" (NIV).

Rest: We Can't Neglect It

After all of this working, we can't neglect resting—especially considering its necessity in the life of the believer. Our physical bodies and minds were simply not designed to "keep pressing for Jesus" at the expense of our sanity. Though God has certainly called us to be faithful and has indeed wired us to work for His purposes—we are not equipped for self-sufficiency. How are we to keep pressing for Jesus if we never press *into* Jesus? Resting in God, or practicing a Sabbath rest, forces us to stop. It deviates our attention off our own agendas allowing us to meditate on the unshakeable character of God. It is quite impressive to realize that God Himself established the Sabbath rest after having sculpted His creation (Genesis 2:2). Though He didn't rest out of necessity (He is God and doesn't get weary), He provides humanity with a blueprint. That is, resting from one's work is essential to the natural order of things (notice that rest comes *after* work). Not only that but resting in God is an opportunity to celebrate! I can only imagine—God probably marveled upon all of His creation on that seventh day, rejoicing in its goodness. What better way for us to reciprocate that celebratory spirit than to marvel in the goodness of our Creator?

What a wonderful opportunity it is to partake in this God-ordained rest. Nevertheless, it does require faith: "For we also have had the good news proclaimed to us, just as they did; but the message they heard was of no value to them, because they did not share the faith of those who obeyed" (Hebrews 4:2, NIV).

When the author of the book of Hebrews uses the word "they" in this Scripture, he is referring to the Israelites. They were unable to enter God's rest due to their disobedience. They had ultimately allowed the deceitfulness of sin to shake their faith in God. As a result, their own hearts were hardened with the cancer of unbelief (Hebrews 3). As believers in the good news of Jesus Christ, we have an opportunity to learn from the rebellion of the Israelites. We can either do as they did, forgetting the faithfulness of God while operating in unbelief and self-sufficiency—or, we can choose to believe God at His Word and rejoice in the rest that only He provides. It's our choice. Either way, God's rest is available to those who want it.

COWARDICE

Naturally, I can be quite the wimp. Some might prefer the phrase "punk." Whichever word suits your fancy—I can very well associate. It was never my goal to be that way though (whose goal is it ever?). The coward-like tendencies just sort of evolved by default. Sometimes, I choose to silence myself when I ought to speak up. Other times, I speak up when I ought to be quiet. I conform though my conscience condemns me. I get assertive about issues that don't matter, yet passive concerning the ones that do. However, underneath my cowardice nature, I have noticed that the root diagnosis of my ailment has always been "people pleasing." That is, doing everything in my power to be accepted, recognized, liked or valued by mere people instead of God. Many people wouldn't dare admit that they embody this mentality—after all, being a coward just isn't a good look. Nobody wants to be that guy in *Titanic* who jumped on the lifeboat when they called for women and children only. I can almost guarantee you, nobody wants to be the suicide bomber on the news who kills himself after murdering a bunch of innocent people. We would much rather take on a Denzel Washington/Will Smith persona. Save the world, stand up for what is right, conquer regardless of the circumstance—you know, be the good guy in every movie. In theory, everyone seeks to be that hero but in actuality, our actions can cosign more so with the profile of the suicide bomber. The reality is ironic.

As a Christian, I know this cowardly condition far too well. Standing up for what is righteous and holy is difficult in a society that outwardly opposes my entire worldview. My battle has always been, "compromise righteousness for the sake of acceptance and face regret and shame" versus "be rejected for the sake of truth and have peace." In all honesty, I have not always taken the righteous, latter approach. Sometimes, my flesh does get the better of me and I do submit to compromise. Though in doing so, I do not always act like a servant of Christ, as I should (Galatians 1:10), I choose to move forward. My past deficiencies don't have to define my future influence. Praise God that slowly but surely, I'm learning that compromise for the sake of people isn't worth my peace of mind. Internal right standing with God is far more satisfying and valuable than being accepted by man on the surface. In admitting these deficiencies in this chapter, I pray that you will not only recognize cowardice tendencies in your own life but through Christ, move forward as well.

Episode 1: The "Tolerant" Christian

(Taken verbatim from my prayer journal)

Lord,

I'm an utter and complete failure. I come short of your glory daily. Daily. I need your saving grace and mercies literally every second of my existence. You sustain me. I'm nothing without You Lord. You've really been showing me my sinful nature lately. Just yesterday, I messed up at work big time. Lesley, Jimmy's friend came in the office talking about Beyoncé at the VMA's. Then, she proceeded to show me a meme of Blue Ivy and Jay-Z saying "My mom is god, which makes me low-key Jesus" or something to that effect. Inside, reading this, I was angry. But I was very conscious to seem approving on the outside—simply shaking my head saying, "that's a shame." That's all I had to say—really! Not only was that a shame, but blasphemous and idolatrous. I seemed approving of an idolatrous, mocking, evil meme—one that totally went against everything I believe in. I then realized I'm a cowardly people pleaser willing to do and say things so that people won't get offended. The only issue with that is that I inevitably offend God—the only One that counts.

I really couldn't believe I had acted that way. I'm a die-hard Christian. I felt like Peter denying Jesus before He was crucified. I felt like scum. Literally, right after it happened, I began to silently weep at my desk. Tears very subtlety ran down my cheeks. I had to excuse myself to the bathroom to sob in repentance. How could I be so double-minded and evil? How could I cosign on a meme that I didn't even like—with celebrities that I definitely don't care for? What was my problem? I could so easily share a blog post about how Jay-Z and Beyoncé typically represent many things, not of God, yet in real life, I had nothing to say except "that's a shame" with a smirk on my face. What in the world! I really can't forgive myself even now Lord. I found myself wanting to die a little bit or at least suffer for the sin I had just committed. But Lord, You already took on that wrath for me on the cross. I don't deserve *it—which is why I'm saved by grace, not merit. You could have taken me out in that very moment like Ananias and Sapphira. Yet, You had mercy on me. You allowed me to breathe and you still have a purpose for my life. That really allowed me to see your gospel for what it really is. The power of God to save. Regardless of the offense. Without condition—You love. Jesus, I love You—and I can't continue to have this people pleasing mentality. If someone doesn't like me so what. I should take it as a compliment because they didn't like You either and no servant is greater than his Master. Jesus, I can't be liked by everybody— nor can I be friends with this world. That means I'm at enmity with You. I can't have that. I can't compromise. Lord have mercy. I don't know how or why this is so hard for me. Lord birth in me a boldness for you. I want to be brave. I no longer want to wallow in disobedience and cowardice. I want to share in Your sufferings and take up my cross. Whether that cross is rejection or whatever, it's worth it. I'm accepted by You. Why isn't that enough for me when it ought?*

Acceptance of people and desiring that will make me crazy because people can't be pleased Lord. You truly are the only one that matters. I absolutely love You for loving me through my weakness—through my cowardly tendencies. I know I will overcome through You Jesus. My God isn't a punk— nor am I. Lord teach me how to be Your ambassador on this Earth. Teach me how to be genuine regardless of the company I keep. Lord, I offer You a heartfelt petition of repentance—and

Lord I know You're faithful to forgive. Your grace is sufficient. Even when I'm flawed. God, redeem me!

Upon studying the character of Peter last night, I realized that I'm a lot like him. Around the disciples, Peter was bold. Walking on water, chopping people's ears off. Doing the most. But as soon as opposition came, he was outside the comfort zone of the saints and his life and reputation were on the line—he denied Jesus, not once, not twice, but three times. I'm no better. I minister with TP, put on this holy facade on social media and am bold with the saints/church folk. But when I face opposition at work and at internships I allow evil to consume me. I conform to "tolerance." It has become an idol in my heart Lord. Cleanse me Jesus. Forgive my wicked heart. Make me NEW.

You might read this journal entry and think, "Why is she so upset? It wasn't even that serious." Or you might be thinking, "Is she crazy, I would never do that!" Either way, I took that experience very seriously because this was not the first time that something like this had happened to me. In my mind, I felt like I was becoming notorious for being too tolerant of sin. Inadvertently, I was consenting to evil simply by being indifferent and/or passive. Love doesn't delight in evil, it rejoices in the truth (1 Corinthians 13:6). Seeming indifferent about something that didn't sit right with my spirit in the first place didn't demonstrate rejection of evil, instead, by default, it implied acceptance.

There was a time in my life when this type of behavior wouldn't have bothered me one bit. I would have laughed at the meme and kept it moving. Though I did submit to my cowardly tendencies in this situation, I do thank God that I at least had the Holy Spirit inside of me letting me know my wrong and leading me towards the things of truth (John 16:13). Apart from the Holy Spirit, I surely would have delighted in evil by not only being indifferent but by being openly accepting of such mockery. Apart from God, I'm plain evil. Though society wouldn't constitute this behavior as evil by the least, that just goes to show that according to society, "truth" is relative and negotiable. According to God, truth is objectively pronounced by Him, and that truth is the only one that matters.

Christian Cowards?

Cowardice, according to the dictionary means lack of bravery. To put it more honestly, it could mean that you're comfortable, complacent or stuck in your ways. Or, you could take it to mean that you're too paralyzed by fear to move forward. Cowardly behaviors come about from a variety of catalysts—more than I could name at this point. I have to ask myself sometimes—"What types of situations prompt me to lack bravery, especially when Christ is supposed to be my hero?" It's understandable for an unsaved person to feel anxiety, worry, and fear—but what's my excuse? Could it be that I don't completely trust Christ like I claim to trust Him? Could it be that

I allow circumstances and people's opinions to deter me from faithfulness? I would have to say "yes" to both. Admittedly so, my mouth sometimes testifies about the goodness and trustworthiness of God, meanwhile, my actions reveal a more atheistic temperament. Sadly, more so than not, if Christians really examined themselves, more of us could relate to this cowardly nature than we think.

That definition really made me ponder from a Christian worldview what a "lack of bravery" means for a Christ-follower. Ultimately, it goes to show that some of us don't truly trust God as we claim. If we did, we would accompany our faith with works (James 2:17). Take the Israelites for example—even after God had brought on plagues, saved their very lives with the blood of a lamb during Passover, parted the Red Sea and delivered them from the hand of their oppressor (the Egyptians), they *still* didn't trust Him. As a result, that generation missed out on seeing the Promised Land because of their constant lack of faith. They even pleaded with Moses to go back to Egypt, where they had been enslaved! Or even worse, back into the wilderness where they could have died! (Numbers 14). All because they relied on their futile feelings in that moment, instead of focusing on the true character of God and realizing that He had their backs the entire time—if only they had believed. Of that generation, only Joshua and Caleb got to see the Promised Land because they trusted God even when confronted by their enemies and death itself. It didn't mean they weren't intimidated or fearful, after all, Scripture says "be strong and courageous" and "do not be afraid" countless times in the book of Joshua because fear is real. Nevertheless, faith is greater. When we begin to discount our fear as futile compared to the greatness of God, that's when God's power is revealed, and our faith is strengthened further.

While I'm on the topic of biblical examples of bravery, and the lack thereof, I'd like to mention that cowardly tendencies in a people sometimes derive from cowardly leadership in a person. Take Aaron, the brother of Moses for example. God had placed Aaron in leadership alongside Moses to appease him in his weakness because Moses was insecure about his speech. In doing so, Aaron was instructed to speak to the Hebrews for Moses, and it was as if Aaron were Moses' mouth and as if Moses were God to Aaron. (Exodus 4:16). This is a huge responsibility for Aaron. He sort of functioned as a conduit relaying the messages of Moses from God to the people (Exodus 7:1-2). Thus, as far as order was concerned—Aaron submitted to Moses' leadership and Moses submitted to God's leadership. This was a system of order put in place by God, mind you, so its very nature was divinely orchestrated and good. In Exodus 32, Aaron decided to defy this order when pressured by the people to sin:

"When the people saw that Moses was so long in coming down from the mountain, they gathered around Aaron and said, 'Come, make us gods who will go before us. As for this fellow

Moses who brought us up out of Egypt, we don't know what has happened to him.'"
(Exodus 32:1, NIV)

So, Moses was on Mount Sinai, talking to God and the people were quite frankly tired of God and the man of God (Moses). They would much rather worship themselves and their own abilities.

"Aaron answered them, 'Take off the gold earrings that your wives, your sons and your daughters are wearing, and bring them to me.' So all the people took off their earrings and brought them to Aaron. He took what they handed him and made it into an idol cast in the shape of a calf, fashioning it with a tool. Then they said, 'These are your gods, Israel, who brought you up out of Egypt.'"
(Exodus 32:2-4, NIV)

Hold up! Did that just happen? Aaron didn't even address the Israelites' foolery. He didn't even tell them they were dead wrong for asking him such a thing. He instead, ejected himself out of his God-ordained role in leadership, in order to be affirmed by the people. Aaron found his way of thinking much more valuable than obedient submission to God and Moses. In Aaron's rebellion, he made a golden calf out of jewelry—all the while having the audacity to think he had *done* something. Not only that—he actually found it appropriate to declare that this golden calf, which didn't exist two seconds earlier, the god that brought them out of Egypt. Was he crazy!? His sins were just piling on top of one another at this point (pride, disobedience, lying, idolatry, etc.). The mess he had gotten himself into was beyond ridiculous. If that wasn't enough, in verse 5, Aaron decided to have a festival unto the Lord God the following day. God gave notice to Moses as to what was going down, and clearly He was full of righteous anger. Moses eventually returned to the camp where the Israelites were dwelling, to ask Aaron why he had led the people into such a great sin:

> *"Do not be angry, my lord," Aaron answered. "You know how prone these people are to evil." (Exodus 32:22, NIV)*

Seriously Aaron. He didn't even take responsibility for his poor leadership. Instead, he blamed his actions on the people and even proceeded to justify it! This is cowardly behavior at its finest because Aaron not only feared the people but when Moses came back he feared him as well (hence, he told Moses not to be angry). Aaron was being swayed in every direction because he was clearly off balance due to his reliance on self, instead of God. He had no foundation to keep him grounded. He had no truth to keep him stable. All the while, the entire people of Israel became the laughing stock of their enemies because Aaron had allowed them to sin in this capacity (Exodus 32:25).

I know it may seem like I'm giving Aaron a harsh critique, but it's only because I can identify with his behavior. Though I've never worshiped a golden calf, I have made idols out of possessions and myself. The Israelites didn't understand that just because they were worshipping an inanimate object in the form of a golden calf, didn't make that object any more legitimate or God any less legitimate. Just because they discredited the one and only true and living God, didn't mean that He didn't exist. After all, humans don't define truth, God does.

At the end of the day, Aaron passively went along with everything the Israelites wanted because he was too concerned with appeasing the opinions and desires of the masses instead of speaking against their sin. Like Aaron, sometimes, I passively condone the sins of others when I ought to be opposing it. Just like in my "tolerant" Christian episode, it is very possible to cosign on something without even saying a word. Just because we might not say outright that we're delighting in the sin of another, that's exactly what we do when remaining passive in some situations.

I can't speak for everyone, but I know that one reason I revert to being passive in these situations is because I'm afraid of offending people. I'm afraid that they will assume I'm a judgmental Christian, and turn them away from Christ. Plus, I know I can appear to be harsh and quite frankly, I haven't perfected that balance of grace and truth, so I use that insecurity as an excuse to remain silent most times. Nevertheless, I know that perfect love drives out all fear because fear has to do with punishment (1John 4:18). Fear of punishment? What punishment? Those are valid questions. Romans 4:15 answers them for us, "For the law always brings punishment on those who try to obey it. (The only way to avoid breaking the law is to have no law to break!)" (NLT). The fact that I'm constantly missing the mark in every area of life because I'm a sinner automatically brings a sense of condemnation. But the perfect love of God through Christ allows me not to fear this punishment anymore because there's no condemnation for those who are in Christ Jesus (Romans 8:1). With that being said, I'm learning day by day that my insecurities concerning speaking the truth ought never to scare me into remaining silent when it isn't the time to be silent.

    I have been in situations where I have opted to stay quiet in fear (and feel guilty after the fact), rather than telling someone the truth about their sin in love. It's almost like refusing to discipline a child. I've never been a parent, but I can only imagine that one might feel some sense of remorse and/or guilt for disciplining their child. I believe that's the reason why some parents would rather skip the discipline altogether and give the child their every waking desire (other than the fact that it's the easier alternative). However, we know this behavior only reaps a spoiled harvest. Discipline is good because in a sense, it defends the truth. If you think about it, the only reason why kids get in trouble in the first place is because they simply deviate from what is true and right. Likewise, when my loved ones deviate from what is righteous in the sight of God, shouldn't I act in love by correcting them? Wouldn't it be wrong of me as a child of God to let their sin slide because I didn't want to upset them? Isn't that selfish of me? Now, I'm not suggesting that we go around condemning people. I'm proposing that we do just what Jesus did—share the truth in love.

Sharing the truth *in love* has been a daunting task for me as of late. I find myself being either too frivolous in my speech or too harsh in my delivery. It's something I've been in prayer about. Sometimes, I get so passionate when correcting someone that I forget about my tone altogether and come off as judgmental. I'll even get defensive when people rebuke me for my tone because I feel justified in speaking the truth. However, I'm learning that I could speak the truth all day, but without love, it will never be received—the whole point of correction is to edify. Without love, I'm just making noise (1 Corinthians 13:1). Sadly, no one will ever hear the melodious truths that are spewing out of my heart to declare if my delivery is off. It's a delicate balance. I also think that although my intentions may be pure, my speech isn't always loving because I'm aware of my cowardly ways. I suppose, in trying to overcompensate for my natural inclination to shrink, I become unnecessarily direct. I share this as a warning. Speaking the unadulterated truth isn't an excuse to be rude and self-seeking, even if we are "being real." Sharing truth is an opportunity to extend the grace of Christ to others.

However, I do want to emphasize that neglecting to share the truth ought never to be an option. Just last night, I caught myself watching a television show about an obese woman and her desire to lose weight. At this point, she was around 600 pounds I believe and on the verge of death. She couldn't even stand, far less walk. She was imprisoned to the confines of her bed and left dependent on her subservient husband. She had absolutely no quality of life. However, what I could not understand is how her husband managed to buy, prepare, and cook greasy fried foods for her even while she was trying to get approved for gastric bypass surgery! He was only doing what she told him to do, but contrary to his thinking, he wasn't helping her in the least. If anything, he was murdering her further by knowing the truth, yet, conforming to her every want and desire. Though the junk food always gratified her initially, it was killing her bite by bite. That's EXACTLY how the devil operates. No offense to the gentleman on the television show, I'm in no way calling him Satan. What I am saying is that the enemy lures us with things that are pleasurable to us. He wraps sin in cotton candy to make for a more enticing exhibit. Though we may be gratified for a moment, he leaves us for dead eternally. Surely, you would agree that there is nothing loving about that scenario. Just like there's nothing loving or glamorous about feeding your wife who is obviously struggling with her food addiction more junk—there's nothing loving about condoning the sins of others.

      Condoning the sins of one another is often done subconsciously because we neglect to hold a standard. This standard that I speak of is truth, and it can't be twisted to pacify our innate sinful nature. Have you ever wondered why truth seems to be relative nowadays? Clouded by the haughtiness of opinion, humanity has exchanged the very Word of God for selfish proclamations. Petrified by anything that deems itself contrary to their complacent, narrow way of thinking—people will instead, invent their own moral compasses. All of this is done in high hopes so people can somehow create this utopian world filled with their own "truths." If only they realized that their playhouse lives were actually self-inflicted prisons of denial. I love how Braille articulates this truth in Beautiful Eulogy's song, "You Can Save Me":

"Can mankind make an image of a god and be convinced that,
The god that they imagined in their mind is a god that exists?
But if God made man, how can man make a god,
And make a claim that God is confined to fit within a frame?
How can mankind decide how God should be identified?
Can you alter the truth if you accept or deny?
Do the stars disappear when the blind look at the sky?
Or do they simply fail to see what was there the whole time?" [1]

Not only is it logical to understand that nothing and no one can taint the unshakeable character of God, but Scripture definitely testifies to this truth: "What if some were unfaithful? Will their unfaithfulness nullify God's faithfulness? Not at all! Let God be true and every human being a liar..." (Romans 3:3-4a, NIV). If God suddenly ceased to be God whenever man had an opinion contrary to His nature, would God be God at all? Think about it—without God's truth, there is no right or wrong. If there's no right or wrong, everything is acceptable. If everything is acceptable, people who do bad things never get punished for them because "bad" is subjective. If there was no punishment, how would justice abide? If no one received justice, people would be livid! People would go around killing people without any consequences (which happens in our society now, but I digress). However, when the tables are turned and we come to find out *we* are the bad people, and *we* are the ones who rightly deserve death because of our sins, justice doesn't sound as rewarding. In fact, I would much rather avoid it all together because it literally sounds like a hopeless, depressing situation to be in.

That's where grace steps in—it's just as important as truth. Minimizing it doesn't do God any justice, and it surely doesn't represent His character well. When I think of this balance of truth and grace, my mind reverts to the gospel every time. Isn't that what God did for us? Because of the fact that we deserve death, God sent His Son Jesus to rescue us from the mess we had gotten ourselves in. But He didn't just let us off "in the name of love" by deeming our sins as forgiven without any punishment for those sins. That would be unlawful of Him—a perfect, just God doesn't just "let people off." Rather, Jesus took our place on the cross by literally paying for the death that all of humanity deserved. Justice married love in that moment. It really was a perfect plan on God's part if you think about it. Justice is satisfied, God's love for us is manifested, and death is swallowed up by victory because Christ is resurrected from the dead at the end of the story! Christ wins and everyone in Him become winners!

What's so sad about this truth is that many of us (including me) are aware of this good news, otherwise known as the gospel. Yet, we continue to live substandard lives insisting that we fade to the background, instead of standing out for Christ in boldness. That's what cowardly people do—they lack bravery because they're afraid of reprimand. We are not cowardly beings. If you are in Christ, the cowardly nature in you never outweighs God's Spirit dwelling inside of you. It doesn't matter what you've done. It doesn't even matter if you've denied Christ in the past—Jesus is the ultimate Redeemer. Just look at Peter, by the grace of God, though he had denied Christ three times, his purpose wasn't revoked. The crazy thing about it all was that Jesus knew Peter would deny Him before He called him. God still used him to build His Church—even though He is omniscient. If Peter had wallowed in his sorrows like Judas and allowed bitterness to overwhelm him into hopelessness, where would the Church be today? After Christ's resurrection, Peter was so amped because he *knew* his sin didn't count against him! He had confidence in *who* Christ was, not in his own abilities because clearly he had failed in every way. Yet, Christ still showered Peter in grace and love, expressing in that moment of resurrection that nothing could keep us from His unrelenting pursuit. There's no reason that we should be afraid of any consequences in Christ. After all, perfect love drives out all fear because fear has to do with punishment. Christ is our perfect love. What do we have to be afraid of when Christ has defeated everything? That kind of hope will absolutely bring confidence to a coward. Peter is a prime example! Upon being persecuted, he actually insisted that he be crucified upside down because he deemed himself too unworthy to be crucified right side up like his Savior. This is the same guy who denied Christ out of fear that he would be socially ridiculed. Ironically, he died as a martyr on a cross—one of the most humiliating public displays of torment imaginable. That transformation of mind and will is possible only through Jesus.

Suffering

Another reason why people conform to cowardice tendencies is because we are fearful of another type of punishment—suffering. We live in a society that has a very low tolerance to pain. Americans typically enjoy things quickly and instantly. The only issue with that state of mind is that we never go through any processes. If you think about it, many things that are aged undergo processes, which allow them to come out stronger and better after it's all said and done. Wine is enhanced when aged, meat is more flavorful slowly cooked, caterpillars evolve into butterflies—we learn these principles in kindergarten (well, maybe not the wine part). Though this logic should resonate fresh in our minds because they're so elementary in nature, we as a society understand processes in theory—yet avoid them like the plague experientially. I know I am guilty. God always has a way of snatching us up when it comes to experiential resistance in order that we can evolve in the processes necessary to becoming better. We will never be better if we always advocate for the easy way out. Since God is good, and He's on our side, He wants us to be better.

If you classify yourself as a coward and desire a courageous spirit—God desires for you to grow up in your salvation. You just might have to endure the fire first. 1 Peter 1:6-7 says it best, "In all this you greatly rejoice, though now for a little while you may have had to suffer grief in all kinds of trials. These have come so that the proven genuineness of your faith—of greater worth than gold, which perishes even though refined by fire—may result in praise, glory and honor when Jesus Christ is revealed" (NIV). Isn't it reassuring that God Himself considers your faith so precious that He allows it to go through the fire in order to be truly refined? If mere gold can go through the fire to be cleansed of all its impurities for worldly consumption, how much more is it necessary that our faith endures the same treatment for the sake of godliness?

Surely, going through the fire is no easy venture. You will have to endure the scorching heat. You might feel the burdens of life so much so, that you begin to suffocate. You might even come out with second and third-degree burns from your time spent in the furnace—but after you come out, you're purged of former impurities and more equipped for the journey ahead. All the while, you come to realize that Jesus was with you the entire time—protecting and nurturing you through the very flames you once thought would consume your life.

As I began writing about the subject of suffering as it relates to bravery, I immediately thought of two things—my sister in Christ and the persecuted church. My sister in Christ, Raven, is also one of the most courageous people I have met. She truly embodies the essence of Proverbs 31:25—"She is clothed with strength and dignity, and she laughs without fear of the future" (NLT). Though at twenty-three she has battled sickle cell anemia and Crohn's disease for some time now—one would never know because she refuses to let it define her. Her quiet strength and tender heart for Jesus forever testifies that she is an overcomer. That victorious spirit of hers radiates, even without her saying a word. I am personally encouraged by her press, especially because she's so young— I think we all could learn a thing or two from her. She's a living testimony that even through the pain and frustration of suffering, it is never in vain.

Suffering always acts as a vehicle for God's glory. Not only that, but I can tell that she has, in turn, known Christ more deeply because of her condition. I'm positive that every IV, every ounce of blood drawn, every surgery, every transfusion, every fatigued day—all of it, was worth knowing Christ in an increasingly intimate measure. Paul indeed said it best: "What is more, I consider everything a loss because of the surpassing worth of knowing Christ Jesus my Lord, for whose sake I have lost all things. I consider them garbage, that I may gain Christ and be found in him, not having a righteousness of my own that comes from the law, but that which is through faith in Christ—the righteousness that comes from God on the basis of faith. I want to know Christ—yes, to know the power of his resurrection and participation in his sufferings, becoming like him in his death, and so, somehow, attaining to the resurrection from the dead" (Philippians 3:8-11, NIV).

Upon watching an interview of a young man whose two brothers were brutally beheaded because they failed to denounce Jesus as Lord, I was immediately captivated and convicted simultaneously. Not only was I allured by the faith of these brave martyrs, but I was also taken aback by the resolve of the martyrs' younger brother who was being interviewed. In the midst of flames and seemingly unbearable loss, he was not only proud of his brothers for proclaiming Christ unto death, but he was also thankful that the beheading served as a gateway for his brothers to see eternal life in heaven. What kind of kingdom mindset this young man had to deem everything of this life as insignificant compared to life in Christ. This man's faith had been proven to be genuine—not because he talked about being faithful, but rather that his faithfulness was evident in the manner in which he lived, even during one of the most trying seasons of his life.

What excuses then, do those of us who deem ourselves cowardly have? I'm learning that people will continue to make a mockery out of our God, our faith, and the truth, simply if we allow them to. Tolerating everyone's foolishness is not the approach we ought to take to win souls for Christ. The world seems to be accentuating its darkness in desperation for the brightness of light. Meanwhile, we as Christians dim our lights for the sake of tolerance in the world. The world is checking for our righteousness, and we're checking for their acceptance. We cannot merely "coexist" as the bumper sticker suggests—we *must* be brave.

A Call to Bravery

"On the day I called, You answered me; You made me bold with strength in my soul." (Psalm 138:3, NASB)

Have you ever taken pride in your association with a particular person or organization? I have. Growing up, I always reminded people that I was related to my older sister, Whitney. I wanted to emulate her, raid her conversations, play with her, and look like her. Ironically, now that we're older my wish has unfortunately come true and people now mistake us for twins. In retrospect, I think God in His foreknowledge (and sense of humor) did that on purpose—but I digress. The point is, that I valued my sister so much that I was even willing to take pride in being her shadow as a child. How much more should we take pride in God as His children? And He doesn't even deem us as mere shadows (although that would be an honor and privilege). He deems us as friends (John 15:15). It is encouraging to know that I can be brave for Christ's sake knowing that a.) He's my friend b.) He was brave for me first.

One song that never ceases to amaze me in this season of my life is "You Make Me Brave" by Bethel Music. I've almost adopted it as my anthem because all my life, bravery has never been a strong suit. I've always faded into the background; refusing to entertain the convictions raging inside of me and stand up for what was right. Jesus, however, overshadows me. He shows me that He is greater than any punishment, any insecurity, any weakness, any frailty, any excuse, any lie, any reputation, and any person. Though I'm not perfect, I'm so glad that Jesus gives me the strength to overcome fear with faith regardless of the circumstance. Certainly, if He can give me that kind of confidence in the midst of my boundless mess-ups and failures—He can definitely equip you with assurance just the same. "You make me brave, You make me brave, You call me out beyond the shore into the waves. You make me brave, You make me brave, no fear can hinder now the love that made a way." [2]

Good Girl Gone Brave

Why is it imperative to be brave? Why isn't it just enough to be a good Christian girl—one who's kind, generous, and overall pleasant? Acquiring these attributes is all well and dandy, but they're not biblical. For one, our goodness does not come from ourselves. It's not merely enough to be nice and kind, as if those qualities could ever translate into goodness in the first place. Jesus said Himself, only God is good (Mark 10:18). Our weak attempts to allure people into liking our sweet flawless facades are in vain. Do you really desire to be good? It would be courageous and honest of you to first, address that you're sinful. Believe me, I've been there. I really thought it was enough to be "nice" so that everyone would like me. This cost me my integrity. I wanted so desperately to be accepted and valued. But what I failed to realize is that niceness (just for the sake of being nice) comes with a consequence, it's called—compromise. It's simply impossible to please everyone and be true to yourself at the same time.

As the saying goes, "If you don't stand for something, you'll fall for anything" but it's not enough to stand for just something. If you stand for anything, you'll fall for anything just the same. You must stand for Christ and Christ alone to survive in a world full of compromise. What I have realized is that when I choose to unashamedly stand for Christ, people always have something negative to say (John 15:18). It's a part of the territory. In knowing that ahead of time, I'll take my enemies and naysayers for Christ. He never compromised once for me even though He had every right to do so. He unapologetically died like a wretched sinner for my sake. The least I can do is be brave for Him.

Though I haven't been as courageous as I would have desired to be in the past, I'm a living testament that God doesn't throw you away even after an epic failure. If Christ in His foreknowledge made Peter a martyr for His glory, even in knowing that he would eventually deny Him three times, that gives me the assurance that He does the same thing for me. He knew my sins of cowardice before one even manifested; yet, He still called me to a life of purpose. The same holds true for you. There's no point of wallowing in your failure when God wants to redeem that same failure you have written off as hopeless for His glory. Dare to let your former cowardice tendencies be a testament to the redemptive power of Christ.

DOUBT

Most people understand that doubt displeases God. Hebrews 11:6 addresses that; "And without faith it is impossible to please God, because anyone who comes to him must believe that he exists and that he rewards those who earnestly seek him" (NIV). Although intellectually, I have a concrete understanding that doubt displeases God and is indeed a sin (Romans 14:23) sometimes it seems as if my actions haven't quite caught up with my brain.

It seems as if all my life, I've operated in fear and doubt, which in turn, has brought on anxiety. Does God really love me? Is His grace actually sufficient? Is it enough just to have faith? These kinds of thoughts occasionally wreak havoc on my mind. It's almost like by worrying, I have convinced myself that my condition is permissible because it just showcases how much I *really* care. God wants me to care, right? Ironically, it only displays my lack of faith, which is so incredibly displeasing to God.

For example, while writing this book one day, my USB I had been saving my manuscript on decided that it wanted to vanish while I was at work. I had approximately fifty-five pages or so written at that time. All smart writers know to have a backup, which is why I had saved a previous version of the manuscript to my Google drive a week or so prior. However, I was still hysterical because the latest version of my writing was no longer accessible to me. I was so confident that I left the flash drive on my kitchen table, but when I returned from work that afternoon, it was nowhere to be found. I started praying, asking

God to allow this USB to show up. After all, I was just trying to do what He told me to do in the first place! So, I'm in my house praying up a storm, praying crazy prayers like "God just open my eyes to the USB!" "Make it appear somewhere," "Lead me to where it is God." I eventually gave up in frustration after some time had passed. I began to think, "Maybe this isn't God's will for me to write this." "Maybe it's a sign that I should stop." *Boom!* just that quickly, my faith had been shaken all because of one measly circumstance.

      Surprisingly, a week later, I found my USB conveniently lying on the floor of my car, right by the driver's side door. I was ecstatic! God didn't revoke my assignment from me! My purpose had resurfaced! But then I began to think—*why did I have so little faith to begin with*? Like come on, it was just a USB that was already saved onto another drive. How did I allow myself to become so consumed by this one situation? After all, does the character of God shift because my world shifts? It was like I had limited God so much so, that a trivial USB had become bigger than Him in my mind. I had begun believing the *lies* in my head over the truth. My thoughts were so jacked up—I was almost acting as if I were spiritually schizophrenic. On one hand, I was flirting with the lies of the enemy, and on the other, I was trying to believe God. It was like I had to make up in my mind to trust God wholeheartedly, or believe the lies fully. There wasn't any middle ground. God didn't take pleasure in my wishy-washy, lie-infested mentality.

Sadly, this happens more often than I would like in my everyday life. Though I can only account for my experiences, I can only imagine how many self-proclaimed "good girls" go through this very same mental battle. In thinking our way is best, at times, we can esteem our feelings more highly than God's Word—the ultimate source of truth. When I choose to believe me over Scripture, I willingly give the enemy a license to deceive me. And if my mind is deceived, my heart isn't too far behind.

From a different perspective, doubting God has been the culprit behind me sinning in other ways in the past. Take lust for example. For the longest time, I believed the lie that it was permissible to hopscotch around intercourse by doing every other raunchy act conceivable. But—that is a lie! How is it that I can so clearly identify that lie now, but at one time I was so blinded? Back then, I placed my feelings on a higher pedestal than God. Even though God was a part of my decision-making process, (a minimal part, but a part nevertheless) truth always took a backseat to the raging lusts warring over my heart. I refused to believe that He was able to fulfill me in *better* ways than lust ever could.

Likewise, as it relates to doubt, we must realize that God is *better* than fear of the unknown. Faith in Him as He intends for us to have is *better* than panic and worry. And believe me— I'm most definitely speaking to myself on this one as well. I'm *too* acquainted with panic and worry, so much so, that I have begun to recognize its symptoms. For one, I have noticed that I become frazzled. I cease to make logical decisions altogether.

A prime example of this happened about a year ago. I was in downtown Tampa on my way to a training session for a social advocacy program. It was a Saturday morning, and I was already about forty-five minutes late because I originally went to the wrong location. Apparently, I neglected to thoroughly read an email I received earlier in the week clarifying the location details. All the while, I was debating whether I should quit the training altogether because I felt like I wasn't stable enough to be an advocate to the degree I wanted at that particular season of my life. So, at this point I'm late, I'm frustrated, and I'm angrily driving downtown as a directionally challenged individual. Somehow, in the midst of my hysteria, I decide to illegally turn left in front of a line of cars going straight while in the right lane! Why? Because there was a vacant parking spot available close to the building. A car was centimeters away from hitting me. And to top it off, I also obnoxiously honked at them in response (as if they were in the wrong). I couldn't believe I had almost gotten myself into an accident all because of worry. As I finally parked safe and sound, I just had to relieve myself by crying. I was crying because I needed to spend time with God, I was late, God had graced me through that entire incident, and I was confused about continuing in the program. It was a mess. Through it all, it was almost a sweet reminder to me that God knows, God cares, and

God is working. How arrogant of me to think that I could carry my burdens (though seemingly minuscule from an outside perspective) on my own?

Double-Minded Catalyst

I am learning that the evolution of my doubt, fear, anxiety, and worry ultimately derives from double-mindedness. James 1:5-8 says, "If any of you lacks wisdom, let him ask God, who gives generously to all without reproach, and it will be given him. But let him ask in faith, with no doubting, for the one who doubts is like a wave of the sea that is driven and tossed by the wind. For that person must not suppose that he will receive anything from the Lord; he is a double-minded man, unstable in all his ways" (ESV). When I doubt God's Word and deem my emotionalism more trustworthy than God, I do nothing but participate in my own demise.

This type of language that James used in regards to doubt reminds me of Jesus calming the storm in the boat with the disciples. As Jesus and the disciples were crossing the Sea of Galilee, a violent storm arose.

> "And a great windstorm arose, and the waves were breaking into the boat, so that the boat was already filling."
> (Mark 4:37, ESV)

Just as James writes about being "driven and tossed by the wind" figuratively, as it relates to double-mindedness—Mark provides us with a vivid illustration of how this looks literally. The waves of the sea were literally being "driven and tossed by the wind" ultimately causing the disciples to fear for their lives:

> "But he was in the stern, asleep on the cushion. And they woke him and said to him, 'Teacher, do you not care that we are perishing?'"
> (Mark 4:38, ESV)

The disciples were hysterical at this point so they decided to go to Jesus. We know that the disciples already had some level of belief just by the fact that they went to Jesus in the first place. They were aware that Jesus could potentially alter their circumstance. However, in going to Jesus, they combated that existing belief with doubt by asking if He cared whether or not they were perishing. How could they go to Jesus for help, yet ask Him if He cared based on the assumption that they were already perishing? It's almost as if they obtained an unclear understanding of the character of Jesus. In their minds, Jesus didn't care that they were already perishing (since He was sleeping); yet, they still had hope that He would save them, which is why they woke Him up in the first place. The disciples were indeed unstable because they didn't know what to believe.

It didn't make sense to them—how could Jesus be sleeping while they were dying?

"And he awoke and rebuked the wind and said to the sea, 'Peace! Be still!' And the wind ceased, and there was a great calm. He said to them, 'Why are you so afraid? Have you still no faith?'"
(Mark 4:39-40, ESV)

The waves that were threatening the disciples' lives were no match for Jesus. He spoke peace to the elements and it was so. At the end of the day, the question wasn't if Jesus cared about the disciples in their distress. The question was: Why had they been distressed in the first place? Had they not fully comprehended who exactly Jesus was?

This account speaks volumes to me because as much as I would like to say that I would have been faithful in this situation—I absolutely know that Jesus would have needed to resuscitate me because I would have fallen completely out. In knowing my response already, I have to ask myself the same question Jesus asked the disciples—"Why am I so afraid?" Not just in regards to this hypothetical scenario, but in life. Why do I find myself lacking faith so often? I think it's a combination of things but in all honesty, I think my diagnosis parallels with the disciples', I don't fully understand the character of God. If I did, trusting Him wouldn't be such an issue.

Jesus Cares

"Jesus loves me this I know, for the Bible tells me so, little ones to Him belong, They are weak but He is strong. Yes, Jesus loves me!" Everyone knows the song, but sometimes, I can't wrap my brain around it. Jesus loves *me*. Surely, I can comprehend John 3:16—"For God so loved the world that he gave his one and only Son, that whoever believes in him shall not perish but have eternal life" (NIV). I get that God loved "the world" in this abstract, distant kind of way—but to know that God loved each individual person of "the world," including me, never ceases to amaze me. The fact that He was thinking about me on the cross, that He took the nails, the lashes, the excruciating pain—for *me,* reveals a lot about Jesus' character to say the least. Not only does Jesus love me, but He cares. He didn't love me once on the cross just to throw me away. Rather, He loved me on the cross just so He could love me forever. If that doesn't exhibit His care, I don't know what will.

As I get older, I am learning to appreciate care. Care examines the details; it makes every effort to study the specifics. Care is intended, it doesn't act on a whim, rather, it's meticulously planned and perfectly executed. Care acts out of sheer delight for the well-being of another, not out of obligation. It also thrives in sacrifice. I value care to the extent that I do because a lot of people's version of "care" is watered down (including my own at times). In a society where people behave kindly, spontaneously and/or out of their own convenience, I find truly caring individuals to be a rarity.

To know that Jesus loves me, and chooses to demonstrate this love through His care, is all the more reason for me to trust Him. I believe that the disciples questioned Jesus' level of care for them because of the fact that He was sleeping. How could Jesus sleep as they were facing their demise? And why was He so lax about everything, did He fully grasp the severity of their current predicament? Well of course, in retrospect, we recognize that yes, Jesus was aware of everything, but sometimes, we neglect to emphasize the level of care that He had in this account.

"On that day, when evening had come, he said to them, 'Let us go across to the other side.' And leaving the crowd, they took him with them in the boat, just as he was. And other boats were with him."
(Mark 4:35-36, ESV)

Before Mark's account even begins to develop, we see that Jesus is the one who suggested that they [Jesus and the disciples] go to the other side of the sea. Surely, if Jesus suggested it, we can rest assured that this isn't some spontaneous venture. Jesus in His omniscience knew everything that was about to happen. There was a meticulous plan and purpose preconceived behind the scenes. Jesus not only allowed, but He also *ordained* that storm to occur intentionally.

Some might assume that ordination to be uncaring. Why would Jesus purposefully scare the disciples half to death with a life-threatening storm? What purpose does that scheme hold? Plenty! It not only showcased the disciples' irrational fear, but it also illuminated Jesus' radical care and faithfulness to them—even in the midst of their doubt. Unfortunately, sometimes it takes a storm for us to really understand that God is who He said He is and His character is unwavering, even when we aren't.

Storm aside, Jesus also exhibits incredible care in this account by crossing the Sea of Galilee in the first place. Clearly, He wasn't going to cross the sea aimlessly. He had a definitive destination in mind—and that was Gerasenes. We see in chapter 5 of the book of Mark, how after crossing the sea Jesus went on to heal a demon-possessed man. Jesus cared so much about the character of the disciples and the livelihood of this decrepit man, that He used one journey to accomplish two purposes. How amazing and intentional is that? There's no reason for us to ever doubt a God who cares so much about us that He would orchestrate an entire production starring the wind and waves purely for our edification and His glory!

How amazing is it also that God knew humanity's need for salvation before sin even manifested itself on the earth? He had this brilliant plan to redeem humankind even before creating Adam and Eve, which means that He knew that man would rebel against Him, and would consequently need to be redeemed, yet He created them *anyway* (Genesis 3:15). God is insanely in love with us to do such a thing. A self-sufficient God certainly doesn't need humans for anything. In knowing that, it's incredible to realize that He *wanted* us. Us—the dust-formed, mortal wanderers of the earth, who with sin—tainted the very image of God. Yup, He wanted us so much so, that He wouldn't dare allow sin to get in the way of our communion with one another. He relentlessly pursued us, even unto death. Regardless of life circumstances and feelings that may attempt to convince us otherwise, it's vital to know that God has proven His radical love and care for us since the beginning of time. And nothing or no one can ever change that—not even us (Romans 8:38-39). Renewing our minds on how much God really cares about us regardless of how it may seem, will help us to better understand His character, and as a result—eradicate doubt in our hearts.

Jesus > Life Circumstances

"...Here on earth you will have many trials and sorrows. But take heart, because I have overcome the world"
(John 16:33, NLT)

I know many times, I've been likely to doubt when my interpretation of what reality should be varies from God's ultimate reality. When things don't immediately go my way, or God doesn't show up in the manner that I want Him to, doubt typically takes my mind hostage. I have learned that I usually go through a range of emotions when this happens, and God always seems to be unbothered by all of them. Not to say that God doesn't care, because clearly that's a lie—but it's almost like He allows me to go through my emotional rampages so that I can come to the end of myself, and ultimately replace my futile sentiments with His unfailing truth. When I finally get tired of catching a hissy fit, which always seems perfectly justified at the time, it's as if God meets me where I'm at, just to ask me—"Are you done?" I know that when I'm done magnifying my feelings, God can reveal Himself to me more clearly and as a result, trump my current reality with the infinite, mind-blowing reality of Himself.

Disappointment is a REAL ordeal, and a particular sentiment that I've recognized has propelled me to doubt in this current season of my life. It's as if I have faith in God to do something, and when it doesn't happen as I had imagined it, I become disappointed and consequently stop trusting God as I should. However, it's clear that when this happens, my faith is anchored in a particular circumstance and/or opportunity instead of Christ. If it *had* been appropriately anchored in Christ, I wouldn't be shaken. It's an unfortunate reality for many of us, yet, a reality nonetheless. After experiencing disappointment at a variety of levels, I have learned a very important lesson— God cannot be manipulated. I cannot merely bully God into doing something that I feel is pertinent. I can petition and tell the Lord my desires, but at the end of the day, I must rest in the fact that His will be done—even if it's contrary to my own.

In realizing all of this, I can rest assured in the fact that God is for me and He knows what He's doing. He sees what I can't see, He knows what I don't know—nothing takes Him by surprise. He knows the intricacies, curveballs, and trials of my day-to-day life (Psalm 139:16). Certainly, He knew all my days before one came to be. Likewise, He's also intentional about the victories, triumphs, and glory that I will experience just in the privilege of knowing Him. Whether in victory or in suffering— God chooses to use all of life's circumstances for our good, if we love Him (Romans 8:28). What better journey than to walk confidently with the Lord—unaware of what lies ahead, yet secure in the fact that He has it all together *especially* when we don't. Doubt robs us of the satisfaction and joy that comes with walking with the Lord. It persuades us into thinking that God's ways are unsteady, and therefore, thrusts us into a catastrophic realm of anxiety and insecurity unnecessarily. Even if my worst fear does happen, even if my enemies do consume me, even if I am persecuted, even if I am laughed at, even if I am rejected—I can still have confidence in the Lord. Understanding that God has the wisdom to administer justice as He sees fit and that He's ultimately in control makes all the difference. Even when I meet death face to face, I can still rejoice because it's only a doorway to Jesus. Thus, when I insult the Lord by doubting, it's as if I'm saying that I can trust Him with my soul, but trusting Him in my day-to-day affairs is too burdensome for Him. It's as if to say that He can do the impossible by conquering death, yet, He's too finite and limited in resources to give me something as minuscule as a job. Lord, help us with our double minded mentalities.

A Life Well Worried is a Life Well Wasted

I can't pretend to know anyone else's struggle as it relates to doubt. "Good girl" or not, I can't account for anyone else's experiences except for my own. Fortunately for you, I have enough doubtful scenarios to go around.

From the time I was a young girl, worry, fear, and anxiety have always been a part of my temperament. Before Christ, I never had peace. It didn't matter if everything seemed to be going well—I could still be warring in my mind. Simply put, I didn't trust God with my future, or my present for that matter. Trusting God with my past wasn't any different. I remember stressing about getting arrested for stealing a pack of gum as a child, which I vaguely recall having stolen maybe six years prior—mind you. I was certain that the surveillance cameras had caught me, and I would see myself as a fugitive on the news one day. Guilt over the most minute, insignificant things would torment me. I can also recall stressing over the course of an entire weekend because I didn't know how to tell my "friend" that I didn't like the fact that she talked during movies in elementary school. I had officially acquired the title of a "dweller." In retrospect, I was absolutely ridiculous for thinking as I did, but at the time, it was warranted.

The point being, that although I had read the infamous "worry" chapter (Matthew 6) countless times in my *Precious Moments Children's Bible*, I never understood how God could really and truly take my burdens away from me. I couldn't conceive how someone I couldn't see would provide for me and love me beyond my capacity to bear. I was convinced that my worry and doubt would somehow prove to God my concern, showing Him how serious I was about the things that went on in my life. It seemed to me that if I neglected to worry altogether, it would appear as if I had no concern for my well-being, and how could God be pleased in that? Didn't He want me to care?

My illogical thought processes eventually trickled into adulthood. For that reason alone, college was quite the adjustment. Walking down the pavement of USF's campus for the first time during a weekend "tour" (that was spontaneously orchestrated by my dad) would have been exhilarating for the average high school kid. But in my case, I was holding my breath. Holding my breath in uncertainty, holding my breath in excitement, and holding my breath in confusion. Allow me to elaborate on the third "holding my breath"—for a directionally challenged individual such as myself, walking around a huge college campus (unadvised) for the first time can be quite thrilling (in the worst kind of way), thankfully I survived. It was as if while taking this "tour" I could feel the weightiness of the shift that was about to commence in my life. Seasons were changing, and I didn't know how to feel. It was at that point that I could no longer rely on my family to be my security. I knew I had to rely on God, but I didn't know how that looked realistically. Being that I had allowed doubt to pervert my mind for practically my entire life up to that point, I couldn't comprehend how to trust God, but I knew it was necessary.

Needless to say, that was one of the most enjoyable seasons of my life to date! God really drew me to Himself ever so gradually, yet strategically. He became so valuable to me because He was all I had. Granted, my best friend and I did transition to USF together, however, our friendship in and of itself brought on its own host of challenges. So in the event that we got in a dispute (as we were roommates), the only person I could really confide in was God. I learned to share with Him the most delicate, fragile issues of my heart. Even while I was straddling the fence in my relationship with Him, He continued to pursue me in my resistance. Two college ministries and an incredible church home later, God had affirmed that He was in control of my life, and I was actually excited about it. Regardless of how I felt prior to entering college, God had really assured me that He alone is faithful, and would continue to sustain me through it all.

Though that season was awesome, God never ceases to challenge my faith in a variety of unpredictable ways. It's as if His goal is to constantly outdo Himself, as He always refines me by means of situations that trump my last faith hurdle conquered. I can never get comfortable or ever fathom "arriving" because of this. Certainly, if God's plan is to refine my faith because it's more precious than gold, everything I go through in this life holds purpose. I can be confident in the fact that since God has called me to Himself (John 6:44), He's making me more like Him in the process. "And we all, with unveiled faces, contemplate the Lord's glory, are being transformed into his image with ever increasing glory, which comes from the Lord, who is the Spirit" (2 Corinthians 3:18, NIV). If I'm constantly being transformed into the image of the Lord, then that includes every component of His character—even His faithfulness. Doubt cannot abide alongside faith.

For this reason, chronic doubters like me can be thankful that we're not in this alone. Doubt is real, but sanctification is realer! Those of us in Christ can find relief in knowing that though we may be innately fearful, doubtful, and worrisome now—God is in the transforming business and everything that we go through in this life is being used to transition us from tainted canvases to perfected masterpieces.

Nevertheless, we still have a significant role to play in all of this. God's sovereignty is not an excuse for us to passively sit back and lazily "surrender" our idle lives thinking that change will happen as a result. How can we possibly desire to acquire faithfulness if we never look to the One who is by nature—faithful? How can we look to the One who is faithful without reading Scripture? And how can we read Scripture without believing that we are reading the very words of God?

After all, "All Scripture is God-breathed and is useful for teaching, rebuking, correcting and training in righteousness, so that the servant of God may be thoroughly equipped for every good work" (2 Timothy 3:16-17, NIV).

In this fight against doubt, it is imperative that we as women especially, take every thought that we may have in these imaginations of ours captive, that we may obey Christ as a result (2 Corinthians 10:5). We can't possibly do this unless we have knowledge of God. It makes it utterly hard to know God when we don't spend time with Him, especially in His Word. After all, Scripture is His revelation of Himself to humanity. I'm pretty confident that if I had studied Scripture a little more and actually believed what I read enough to apply it—I wouldn't be struggling with doubt like I do at times.

Sometimes, I'm just too stuck on the situation at hand to care about what God has to say about the matter quite honestly. Far too many times have I attempted to pray and read my Bible in the name of faith while simultaneously doubting and wondering—"God how are you really going to come through?" "Is this a waste of time?" "Do you even hear me?!" At times like this, I just have to remind myself that God's Word is true, He's faithful, and I'm either going to believe it or not. There's no swaying in between—without faith, it's impossible to please God because whoever comes to Him must believe that He exists and He rewards those who earnestly seek Him (Hebrews 11:6). I believe John Piper said it best, "If the Bible's not having an effect on your emotions, it's because you have little faith in what it says."

Episode 2: The Desperate Christian

Lord, I need help. Thankfully, Psalm 121 reminds me that my help comes from You. I'm not self-sufficient, nor can I manipulate You into having my way. You are my help alone and that's what I have to realize. Though circumstances (my mind, my feelings) try to convince me that You're not there and You don't care, Your Word says differently. God help me to believe Your Word as truth. I've been churched all my life and I'm done with emotionalism. I need truth, real revelation, real repentance, and real faith. God, though I'm weary in my faith, God, I'm asking You to be my help. I'm writing this down so I can rejoice when You come through for me. Lord, I know that You're in constant pursuit of my heart, but my heart seems so far from You right now. I know because I know what it's like to experience Your authentic, undeniable peace and joy. I know what it's like to be consumed in Your presence. I know what it's like to connect with Your heart. Which makes the situation worse. How can I know of these things—yet no longer experience You in those ways? Lord, BURN a fire in my heart that can't be tamed. Make me do my part in this as well (keep seeking You) because You're faithful to <u>help</u> and do exactly what you said You're going to do. God, I hate just going through the motions and feeling "blah." Renew the joy of my salvation. Help

140 Doubt

me to enjoy the life that You have given to me. Remind my heart of Your promises when it so desperately wants to stray...

IRRITABLITY

"Don't touch me!"
"Go away."
"Leave me alone."
"You get on my nerves!"
"Are you serious!?"
"What were you thinking?"
"Bruh."

    I never considered these responses sheer evidence of an irritable heart. Heck, even if I had truly understood my condition, it never registered to me that irritability was that big of a deal in the first place, far less a sin. After all, I was just reacting to everyone else's deficiencies. They were the ones with the problems, not me. My preferences were served as the standard that they so conveniently refused to uphold. Only a fiery reaction to such careless behavior would be appropriate. This had been the justification for my irritability, one that I held onto with pure stubbornness.

    According to the *Merriam-Webster Dictionary*, irritability is simply defined as "the quality of easily becoming angry or annoyed."[1] Like I mentioned previously, it was difficult for me to come to terms with my irritability (because it's just not a good look). It wasn't until I had lived with my best friend for one year in college and my sister three years after, that I discovered how easily annoyed I could actually get. I was a true ambassador for Christ outside the four walls of my home. Upon returning home, I found myself hurting those dearest to me in the process. How could I extend radical grace to complete strangers all the while appearing graceless and rigid with my sister and best friend? It's something that I struggle with to this day—and to be honest, I wasn't going to address irritability upon writing this book. Not because I hadn't recognized it to be a sin of mine, rather, because I still struggle with it so much so that I didn't want to seem like a hypocrite for writing about something that I haven't yet "mastered." Christ is showing me that I can't always wait until I come out victorious to share my deficiencies. Irritability may be something that I'm consciously working on, but I believe God is getting the glory out of my transparency even as I go through this sanctification process.

Irritability is the Absence of Love

Irritability is not a word explicitly found in several versions of the Bible, however, we know that although we may not always find a specific word in Scripture, that doesn't mean that God doesn't have anything to say about the subject. My thesaurus says that some synonyms of irritability include grumpiness, moodiness, grouchiness, crankiness—even crabbiness (ouch!). I've never considered myself to have any of these characteristics, but of course, those closest to me have a way of showing me things I may have previously been oblivious to. On many occasions, my sisters in Christ have called me out on my irritability in one form or another, and I can't lie and say that I enjoyed their accountability. Though appreciated, their honest yet loving rebukes have had me feeling misunderstood and slightly judged. I wanted to be valued for my intentions while I had unknowingly condemned everyone else for their reckless actions.

One time, not too long ago, my sister and I had gotten into a minor dispute concerning our townhome that we had recently bought together. Tensions quickly rose between us as we were still trying to delegate financial responsibilities, and it was obvious that we managed money differently. I was the uptight budgeter and she was the lax spender. I couldn't figure out why she seemed so nonchalant about her finances and she couldn't understand why I nagged her all the time because of it. In my mind, I had an expectation that she didn't care to uphold, and it hurt. A mutual friend eventually intervened telling both of us in so many words, that we weren't loving each other as it related to this situation. Though I knew I was being irritable, I associated the irritability with my sister's actions, justifying it by saying that *she* made me act this way, instead of taking ownership of my *own* sin. Our friend's comment and counsel illuminated the fact that I had neglected to love my sister as I should, which was why my irritability had quickly resurfaced as a default reaction. Talk about conviction…

> *"Love is patient and kind; love does not envy or boast; it is not arrogant or rude. It does not insist on its own way; it is not irritable or resentful; it does not rejoice at wrongdoing,*

but rejoices with the truth. Love bears all things, believes all things, hopes all things, endures all things." (1 Corinthians 13:4-7, ESV)

Just in this one situation, I neglected to show love in every possible way. I wasn't demonstrating patience by essentially demanding that my sister conform to my ways. In doing so, my delivery wasn't the kindest. By being so concentrated on my own preferences, I was arrogantly insisting on my own way. By keeping a record of her previous wrongdoing, I was harboring resentment in my heart. By refusing to show compassion in her weakness, I had refused to bear all things.

As a Christian, it's a hard pill to swallow when you unknowingly act against everything you represent. Situations like this have shown me that it's mandatory to show love, not just to strangers and associates, but to the people closest to me—even my family and friends.

Irritability can be a Closet Sin

The late Jerry Bridges taught me a lot about the nature of irritability in his book, *Respectable Sins* (which is—might I add, a definite eye-opener). In it he speaks on our likelihood to show our true colors at home, around the people we care about the most. I believe he addresses this tendency most effectively in his "Impatience and Irritability" chapter:

We tend to exhibit many of these sins ["respectable" sins] most freely in the context of our own families. As I have indicated in an earlier chapter, we can put on our "Christian face" outside the home, but with our families, our true character often comes out. This is especially true in the two areas of sin we will look at in this chapter: impatience and irritability.[2]

When I read this, I couldn't agree more and realized how true the statement actually was, especially as it related to my own life! Irritability is a closet sin because we typically become the most irritable around those whom we love the most. We tend to uphold higher expectations for those we love and thus become the most disappointed in these individuals when they fail us. It isn't fair to be graceless in this way—upholding people to a standard that we ourselves are incapable of satisfying. Just like we fail God's righteous standard constantly and need His forgiveness and grace through Christ, we should likewise be gracious to our loved ones when they disappoint us. I should be ashamed for being so easily irritated when Jesus doesn't respond to me in that way when I mess up, nor does he hold my wrongdoings against me (Isaiah 43:25). I am learning that if I can't even exhibit godly love to those I'm closest to, how can I begin to say that the love of God abides within me? How can I even attempt to show love to my enemies if I neglect to show love within the confines of my home?

"Whoever claims to love God yet hates a brother or sister is a liar. For whoever does not love their brother and sister, whom they have seen, cannot love God, whom they have not seen."
(1 John 4:20, NIV)

THE GOSPEL

"Why do bad things happen to good people? That only happened once, and He volunteered."
-R.C. Sproul Jr.

"For I am not ashamed of the gospel, because it is the power of God that brings salvation to everyone who believes: first to the Jew, then to the Gentile." (Romans 1:16, NIV)

I'm guilty. Upon testifying about the sins mentioned in the previous chapters, I admit that I too fall extremely short. The same truths that I have presented to you convict me all the more. I'm not a superhuman Christian who esteems herself above the righteous standard of God. I'm not holier than thou. If anything, I see myself as the opposite. As I've written this book, I approach you as your fellow sister in the faith. In doing so, I pray that you see my heart.

Most importantly, I hope you clearly see the wicked things in my heart. I'm not proud of them by any means, but I do want you to realize that the only "good" thing inside of me is in fact, Jesus. Likewise, if there's any remote goodness inside of you, it also derives from Jesus. Throughout the course of these chapters, I pray that you've recognized that.

It seems as if we are all stuck in one tragic predicament. We harbor this chronic sin illness that some of us have tried to conceal for years with the facade of togetherness and self-righteousness. We sometimes even jump over hurdles in vain attempts to make ourselves appear untainted and blameless.

However, the fact still remains that we're unrighteous sinners at the end of the day. If this is in fact true, how can an unrighteous person ever go back to reverse the sin that made them unrighteous in the first place? Can they ever deem themselves righteous again? The answer is no. It's simply impossible. It's about as ridiculous as a group of politicians branding themselves as trustworthy after having lied throughout an entire election. Without righteousness, we can also conclude that we're not right in the sight of God. If we're not right, certainly we're wrong. If we're wrong, then we're against God. If we're against God, surely we're His enemies (James 4:4). Not one hence of positive thinking, "good vibe," optimism or charisma can bring hope to that dead situation.

Above all else, we need someone to resurrect us from our dead lives. Contrary to popular belief, we're not fundamentally good people in need of self-help tactics and witty psychology—we're dead people in need of real hope from a real God.

Then enters Christ. The King of kings and Lord of lords. The Son of God. God in the flesh. The Lamb of God. The Good Shepherd. Emmanuel. He is the only one who could save us because He is indeed, God (John 1:1). He wasn't just an influential character in history; He wasn't just a good prophet who performed a bunch of miracles. He wasn't an angelic being either, as some dare to proclaim. He is literally God in the flesh (John 1:14)—all man, all God. By understanding the identity of

Christ, we can truly comprehend the gospel for what it is. If Jesus wasn't God—how would He even have the authority to save us in the first place? If our salvation was to prove itself illegitimate, the wages of sin *still* equal death—meaning we have to pay our own wage and die our own eternal death apart from the saving intercession of Christ (Romans 6:23).

Certainly, all of us would have hopelessly stayed in the grave had it not been for Jesus. Jesus died so that we could become righteous in Him and through His resurrection—live. All of humanity is literally afforded the opportunity to switch places with Him. That's what redemption is all about. Jesus died a real death because of our real sin.

However, living in a culture that romanticizes the cross oftentimes taints our ability to truly comprehend the brutality of Jesus' death. In His suffering, Jesus endured physical death by means of the cross. I believe if only we understood just an ounce of the pain Jesus willingly endured, we would be more inclined to see our sin for what it actually is, and in turn, appreciate the gospel with renewed gratitude.

Physical Death

"He suffered physical death, but He was raised to life in the Spirit."

(1 Peter 3:18b NLT)

Although we will never fully understand the pain that Jesus endured on the cross (and prior to), it certainly doesn't hurt to try. I'm always tempted to gloss over the details involving Jesus' death in Scripture. However, I do nothing in this instance except belittle the Lord's sacrifice. How can we ever begin to appreciate grace when in fact, we haven't fully comprehended the punishment we deserved in the first place? Not only that, but we can learn so much more about God's character while also acquiring a deeper revelation of His love, by humbly attempting to understand His sacrifice.

1. Jesus was flogged prior to being crucified.

> *"He [Pilate] ordered Jesus flogged with a lead-tipping whip, then turned him over to the Roman soldiers to be crucified." (Matthew 27:26b, NLT)*

The act of flogging was something serious. Also referred to as scourging, this form of punishment was not execution in and of itself. Though it had the capabilities to very well slaughter someone prematurely, its main priority was to humiliate. Apparently, scourging was so brutal and demeaning that Roman citizens were usually exempt from enduring such torture—even if convicted of a crime. This type of punishment was reserved strictly for social outcasts (slaves and non-Romans).[1] Jesus wasn't even treated like a common criminal in this case. According to the Romans, Jesus could have very well been treated as sub-human for 1.) not being Roman and 2.) claiming to be the Son of God. I can only imagine what kind of excess force the Roman soldiers exerted during this flogging, just to vainly esteem themselves as superior.

Not only was Jesus flogged—but with a lead-tipping whip, otherwise referred to as a flagellum. According to "The Passion of Christ from a Medical Point of View" by C. Truman Davis, to say that the flagellum inflicted serious pain is an understatement:

> The Roman legionnaire steps forward with the flagellum in his hand. This is a short whip consisting of several heavy leather thongs with two small balls of lead attached near the ends of each. The heavy whip is brought down with full force again and again across Jesus' shoulders, back, and legs. At first, the heavy thongs cut through the skin only.
>
> Then as the blows continue, they cut deeper into the subcutaneous tissues producing first an oozing of blood from the capillaries and veins of the skin and finally, spurting arterial bleeding from vessels in the underlying muscles. Finally, the skin of the back is hanging in long ribbons and the entire area is an unrecognizable mass of torn, bleeding tissue. When it is determined by the centurion in charge that the prisoner is near death, the beating is finally stopped.[2]

2. Jesus endured physical pain while being mocked.

> *And the soldiers led him away inside the palace (that is, the governor's headquarters), and they called together the whole battalion. And they clothed him in a purple cloak, and twisting together a crown of thorns, they put it on him. And they began to salute him, "Hail, King of the Jews!" And they were striking his head with a reed and spitting on him and kneeling down in homage to him. And when they had mocked him, they stripped him of the purple cloak and put his own clothes on him. And they led him out to crucify him. (Mark 15:16-20, ESV)*

If the flogging wasn't enough, Jesus had to listen to the mocking insults of mere men. By clothing Him in the color of royalty in an attempt to disprove His authority, the Roman soldiers (and crowd) possessed a ruthless hatred for Christ for no apparent reason at all. What most of us (including me) have likely failed to comprehend, is in conjunction with the spitting and relentless mocking, pain also played a significant role in addition to the verbal abuse:

> The half-fainting Jesus is then untied and allowed to slump to the stone pavement wet with His own blood. The Roman soldiers throw a robe across His shoulders and place a stick in His hand for a scepter. A

small bundle of flexible branches covered with long thorns (commonly used for firewood) are plaited into the shape of a crown and this is pressed into His scalp. Again, there is copious bleeding (the scalp being one of the most vascular areas of the body). The soldiers take the stick from His hand and strike Him across the head driving the thorns deeper into His scalp. Finally, they tire of their sadistic sport and the robe is torn from His back. This had already become adherent to the clots of blood and serum in the wounds and its removal causes excruciating pain just as in the careless removal of a surgical bandage.[2]

3. Jesus *still* submitted to death even after being flogged.

If I were Jesus, I would have gone back to heaven right then and there—because after all, He very well could if He wanted to. In my wicked mind, humanity wouldn't have been worth the torture. I would have been like "You, mere human, attempt to beat and mock me—and I'm supposed to go through with it? I'm the Son of GOD—I created *you*, you really have no idea." Thank God He doesn't process things like I do! I would have gone about the whole ordeal like a victim. Jesus went about it with initiative. As the ultimate pursuer of His bride—He took every lash, endured every sting, and coped with every insult—just for her. It had been God's plan all along. His accusers were just unknowingly posing as instruments in His grand symphony of salvation.

In realizing that Jesus laid His life down voluntarily and no man could ever take it from Him (John 10:18), it makes this part of the crucifixion story that much sweeter. Jesus was faithful to us, even unto death, not because man made Him die—but because He *laid His life down freely.* And surely, His death wasn't any less legitimate just because He's God. As equally human, Jesus felt *everything.* The flogging just operated as a prelude to the grand scheme of events to come.

On His way to the cross, Jesus was so unbearably weak from the flogging that He couldn't even carry His cross by Himself. The soldiers had to recruit help from Simon, a bystander, just so Jesus could make it to Golgotha (Matthew 27:32-33). This illustrates just how severe the flogging had actually been prior to His crucifixion.

4. Jesus didn't take the easy way out.

As the Roman soldiers ruthlessly drilled nails into Jesus' hands and feet, how convenient would it have been for Him to take the shortcut alternative? Isn't that what the majority of us would have done? I would have gladly accepted a pill, shot, beverage—anything that would ease the pain of being crucified. Not to mention, Jesus was fully God and fully human! He could have very well ascended into heaven right then and there. Yet, He did not check in His "God" card to get Himself out of this wretched predicament. In His full-fledged humanity, Jesus desired to feel 100% of the pain endured. Not only that, but He *had* to feel, in order that God's ultimate plan of redemption could be fulfilled. Jesus was offered wine and vinegar/gall to drink (Matthew 27:34). This mixture was intended to serve as a numbing mechanism, purposed to ease some of the torturous pain. Jesus declined. He desired to fulfill the will of the Father at all costs— even if it meant passing up a beverage to pacify His suffering. He willingly drank that full cup of wrath so that we could, in exchange, experience a life in full. His unfailing love for us served as motivation for every sip of wrath consumed. Christ in all of His splendor and excellence finished what He set out to complete, and did so whole-heartedly. Jesus literally became the servant of all, even upon sacrificing Himself, for *humanity's* sake. This is the same humanity that terrorized, whipped, spat on, mocked, stabbed and betrayed Him in the process. "But God demonstrates his own love for us in this: While we were still sinners, Christ died for us" (Romans 5:8, NIV).

Spiritual Ramifications of Sin Paid on the Cross

"About the ninth hour Jesus cried out with a loud voice, saying, 'ELI, ELI, LAMA SABACHTHANI?' that is, 'MY GOD, MY GOD, WHY HAVE YOU FORSAKEN ME?'"

(Matthew 27:46, ESV)

Scripture is clear that the wages of our sin equal death (Romans 6:23). However, what is this "death" that Paul speaks of? Surely, Adam and Eve didn't physically die immediately after sinning in the Garden of Eden. Since God is not a man that He should lie (Numbers 23:19), we know that a death did occur after the Fall—it just wasn't the kind of death that we intuitively think of. After Adam and Eve rebelled against God and birthed sin into the earth, a *spiritual death* commenced—which, by all means, is worse than any physical death. All of humanity became eternally separated from God. Because God is holy, and He does not coincide with anything less than holy, we were disqualified from abiding in His presence forever. Sin blocked us from the glorious, majestic, holy, almighty God we were designed to love and enjoy eternally. As we're well aware as sinners, apart from God, we're bound to malfunction. It was simply not a part of God's will for us to function apart from Him.

Since Jesus died on the cross for the sins of all humanity to reconcile those who would believe back to God, He also had to be forsaken by His Father for our sake. Through the prophesy of Isaiah we know that "...it was the LORD's good plan to crush him and cause him grief" (Isaiah 53:10a, NLT). God The Father deemed the sacrifice of His one and only beloved Son **good** for the sake of our salvation. He was willing to forsake His Son, whom He loved, in order that we could have life! God forsook His Son so that He could be able to proclaim that He will never forsake us (Hebrews 13:5). Now, we can be confident in the fact that nothing could ever separate us from the love of God because Christ already paid for the very thing that originally separated us from Him—sin.

"Who shall separate us from the love of Christ? Shall tribulation, or distress, or persecution, or famine, or nakedness, or danger, or sword? As it is written,
'For your sake we are being killed all the day long;
we are regarded as sheep to be slaughtered.'

No, in all these things we are more than conquerors through him who loved us. For I am sure that neither death nor life, nor angels nor rulers, nor things present nor things to come, nor powers, nor height nor depth, nor anything else in all creation, will be able to separate us from the love of God in Christ Jesus our Lord."
(Romans 8:35-39, ESV)

It Is Finished

"Therefore when Jesus had received the sour wine, He said, 'It is finished!' And He bowed His head and gave up His spirit."
(John 19:30, NASB)

"Jesus called out with a loud voice, 'Father, into your hands I commit my spirit.' When he had said this, he breathed his last."
(Luke 23:46, NIV)

At the proper time, when His work on the cross was fully completed, Jesus released His spirit and died. By Him proclaiming, "it is finished," we know that the wrath of God had been completely satisfied. It was then Christ's appointed time to die—as there was nothing left to be done. However, in knowing all of this, what exactly does the "it" in "it is finished" signify? What did Christ set out to do during His time spent on earth and how did the cross "seal the deal?"

- Christ's completed sacrifice signified finality. Our past, present and future sins were satisfied once and for all.
    - *"For Christ also died for sins once for all, the just for the unjust, so that He might bring us to God, having been put to death in the flesh, but made alive in the spirit..." (1 Peter 3:18, ESV)*

> There is no sin that Christ's sacrifice didn't cover. As a result, those in Christ do not stand condemned.
>> "Blessed is the one whose transgressions are forgiven, whose sins are covered. Blessed is the one whose sin the Lord does not count against them and in whose spirit is no deceit." (Psalm 32:1-2, NIV)
>> "Therefore there is now no condemnation for those who are in Christ Jesus." (Romans 8:1, ESV)

"It is finished" also indicates literal death. Apart from the undeniable truth of God's Word, we know that even from a historical perspective, Christ truly died. This is significant—for if there was no death, there couldn't have been a resurrection from the dead. Surely the Roman soldiers ensured that Jesus was lifeless prior to burial so no one could refute His supposed demise: "...but coming to Jesus, when they saw that He was already dead, they did not break His legs. But one of the soldiers pierced His side with a spear, and immediately blood and water came out" (John 19:33-34, NASB). Matthew Henry put it this way in his commentary on this Scripture:

> A trial was made whether Jesus was dead. He died in less time than persons crucified commonly did. It showed that he had laid down his life of himself. The spear broke up the very fountains of life; no human body could survive such a wound. But its

being so solemnly attested, shows there was something peculiar in it. The blood and water that flowed out, signified those two great benefits which all believers partake of through Christ, justification and sanctification; blood for atonement, water for purification. They both flow from the pierced side of our Redeemer. To Christ crucified we owe merit for our justification, and Spirit and grace for our sanctification. Let this silence the fears of weak Christians, and encourage their hopes; there came both water and blood out of Jesus' pierced side, both to justify and sanctify them. The Scripture was fulfilled, in Pilate's not allowing his legs to be broken, Ps 34:20. There was a type of this in the paschal lamb, Ex 12:46. May we ever look to Him, whom, by our sins, we have ignorantly and heedlessly pierced, nay, sometimes against convictions and mercies; and who shed from his wounded side both water and blood, that we might be justified and sanctified in his name.[3]

- ➢ Christ came to seek and save the lost. This illustration of Christ seeking us in our sin and rebellion, then saving us through His sacrifice, is perfectly displayed on the cross.

> "For the Son of Man has come to seek and to save that which was lost." (Luke 19:10, NASB)
> "But God demonstrates His own love toward us, in that while we were yet sinners, Christ died for us." (Romans 5:8, NASB)

Resurrection Power

"If the dead are not raised, Let us eat and drink, for tomorrow we die." (1 Corinthians 15:32(b), NIV)

From the outside looking in, the events following Christ's death appear ridiculously bleak. I can only fathom the fear, guilt, shame, and hopelessness circulating around Jerusalem. Peter was probably wallowing in his sorrows after having denied his Savior three times. Pilate was most likely trying to attain a clear conscience by any means possible after conforming to the senseless demands of the people. Surely, all anyone could do at this point was wait. Though prophecy had been spoken about this moment centuries prior, everyone was kept from recollecting these truths until the proper time of revelation (Luke 24). Two days reluctantly passed...and finally—the third day gloriously came:

"On the first day of the week, very early in the morning, the women took the spices they had prepared and went to the tomb. They found the stone rolled away from the tomb, but when they entered, they did not find the body of the Lord Jesus. While they

were wondering about this, suddenly two men in clothes that gleamed like lightning stood beside them. In their fright the women bowed down with their faces to the ground, but the men said to them, "Why do you look for the living among the dead? He is not here; he has risen! Remember how he told you, while he was still with you in Galilee: 'The Son of Man must be delivered over to the hands of sinners, be crucified and on the third day be raised again.' " Then they remembered his words." (*Luke 24:1-8, NIV*)

This is the good news of Jesus Christ. The gospel refrains from being labeled as "good" news, however, if Christ never resurrected from the dead. Without the interjection of this momentous event in the timeline of redemption, hope is nonexistent because we are still dead in our sins (1 Corinthians 15:17). But "Blessed be the God and Father of our Lord Jesus Christ! According to his great mercy, he has caused us to be born again to a living hope through the resurrection of Jesus Christ from the dead," (1 Peter 1:3, ESV). Christ is such the Victor! Not only did God miraculously resurrect His Son from the dead—but He resurrects us from the dead as well! After all, we're the only reason Christ died in the first place. He died to bring life to our decrepit lives. He wasn't the one who needed salvation; He came to deliver it to us. Don't you see? Being *in Christ* is the best thing that could ever happen to you!

Everything that Christ has done—you now have access to, solely if you have *faith in Him.*

How tragic would it be if Christ never walked out of that grave? Scripture reveals that our faith is a pointless waste of time had Christ never resurrected: "And if Christ has not been raised, your faith is futile and you are still in your sins. Then those also who have fallen asleep in Christ have perished. If in Christ we have hope in this life only, we are of all people most to be pitied" (1 Corinthians 15:17-19). In these verses, Paul is brutally honest with his audience. Basically, his point is—if we serve a dead Jesus, what's the point? We're still dead in our sins! He's giving nonbelievers permission to pity Christians if this is in fact true. Thanks be to God, it's not! Christ has indeed resurrected, and His resurrection raises us also. "Who then is the one who condemns? No one. Christ Jesus who died—more than that, who was raised to life—is at the right hand of God and is also interceding for us" (Romans 8:34, NIV).

Don't you see how exciting the reality of the gospel actually is!? The gospel isn't just a genre of music or a churchy phrase—it's our very sustenance, the reason why we live. Because Christ lives we are alive too! Because Christ resurrected from the dead, so will we! Those who believe in Christ as their Lord and Savior will inherit all of these things in the kingdom of God. It's a set in stone, done deal. Regardless of what happens on earth, we can have confidence in our eternal life to come with Jesus. Sadly, those who don't accept this free gift of salvation will have to pay their sentence individually and eternally—apart from the saving intercession of God.

The Qualifier

"...The time is fulfilled, and the kingdom of God is at hand; repent and believe in the gospel."
(Mark 1:15b, ESV)

Repentance and belief are necessary for salvation. Although the "good news" of the gospel is inclusive to all, the reality is that "all" will not receive Christ. Though nobody dares to think about such a grim reality, it doesn't keep it from standing as truth. Truth is, Jesus doesn't want anyone to perish (2 Peter 3:9). Unfortunately, there will be some who, even in light of knowing truth, will reject this overflowing, glorious, gift of salvation. I plead with you, don't stand among the unbelieving and unrepentant.

If I can be honest—prior to having a heart-wrenching revelation of the gospel and its implications, I had it all wrong. I was so stuck on being the best I could be and doing things out of religiosity, that I was too blinded to notice that though I claimed to love God, my actions weren't matching up. How could I claim to be a child of God, yet never acknowledge God, never speak to Him or even commune with Him? Salvation was not about repeating the sinner's prayer so I could wear it as a lucky charm without ever living the life associated with one who was justified by Christ, as I once believed. Salvation is really about believing in Christ's atoning sacrifice—believing so much so, that my faith propels me to deny myself, turn from my sin and turn to God. It is by the power of the Holy Spirit alone that enables this to happen. Without grace and the Holy Spirit working in me, I wouldn't have the capacity to "produce fruit in keeping with repentance" (Matthew 3:8).

I do realize that quite frequently in this book I've referenced my fellow Christ followers as "us," and "we"—however I don't want to deceive anyone by using those pronouns. If you have not turned from your sin and changed your mind about your sin (which grieves God and is deserving of death) by submitting to Christ as your Lord and Savior, you are still an enemy of God. Enemies don't reap the same rewards as children, in fact enemies, to put it frankly—perish. "The eyes of the Lord are on the righteous, and his ears are attentive to their cry; but the face of the Lord is against those who do evil, to blot out their name from the earth" (Psalm 34:15-16, NIV). To willingly be on God's opposing team (especially in light of Christ's atoning sacrifice) rightly deserves eternal punishment beyond human articulation or comprehension. Jesus describes some of the conditions in hell in saying that the wicked will be thrown "into the blazing furnace, where there will be weeping and gnashing of teeth" (Matthew 13:50, NIV). Please, I beg you, if you're reading this and don't know Christ (who is the only Way to God), repent and believe in the gospel! Not as a "get out of hell for free card," but because Christ is worth it! His unrelenting love for you while you were still God's enemy should compel you to love Him and hate your very sin that pinned Him to the cross in the first place.

    I would also like to clarify that the gospel is completely outside of us all. It is literally the gospel *of God* (Romans 1). He orchestrated it, He planned it—He brought it to fruition. We didn't wake up one day pleading with God for salvation. He came to us, showing us our need for salvation (the law), then provided us a way to receive that salvation through Jesus (grace). Our works could never justify us. No matter how hard we work for righteousness, we will never attain it outside of Christ. Living under the law and sticking to the commandments is exhausting—not to mention impossible to fulfill. Christ came not to abolish, but to fulfill the law in our place (Matthew 5:17). So that perfect life that we couldn't possibly live, Christ lived for us. That wrathful death that we surely deserved, Christ died for us. That glorious eternal life that we could never conceive because our minds were so clouded by sin, Christ gifted to us. Surely, all that we have isn't by anything that we've done, or could ever do for that matter. All that we have is because of Christ alone. "And if by grace, then it cannot be based on works; if it were, grace would no longer be grace" (Romans 11:6, NIV).

Grace > Sin

"Therefore, since we have been justified by faith, we have peace with God through our Lord Jesus Christ. Through him we have also obtained access by faith into this grace in which we stand, and we rejoice in hope of the glory of God."
(Romans 5:1-2, ESV)

I went on a zip lining obstacle course for the first time the other day. Overall it was a great experience, but in the back of my mind, all I could think about was the possibility of plunging to my death. Periodically, I wondered to myself, "Why am I putting myself through this!" As I was struggling to get through one level of the course, my brother in Christ tactfully reminded me, "You have a harness, you're safe!" He was absolutely right! There was no reason to fear death because the harness was my protection. It was comforting to realize that even if I suddenly slipped and fell—the harness would catch me. I couldn't understand why it took me so long to understand that.

In light of the saving work of Christ, grace can sometimes be difficult to accept—similar to the harness. It's so amazingly revitalizing that the mere fact that it exists is almost too good to be true. How can ALL of the wretched things I've done be forgiven? The pride, the premeditated lust, the vanity, the laziness, the doubt the... (fill in the blank). At times, the weight of my sin is simply overwhelming. I'm tempted to shrink down in despair when it seems as if I can't get anything right.

Sometimes, I literally feel like I'm one sin away from God giving up on me.

Then, I'm always reminded that by faith I am free to stand confidently in grace. Because Christ paid for everything I deserve, He justified me, and as a result I have peace with God! I no longer stand condemned because Christ was condemned in my place! Thus, there's no need to shrink when grace shines its face upon me. Instead, I can smile knowing that Jesus sees me, He knows me and *yet*, He still loves me!

I was listening to a sermon by John Piper the other day; it was entitled "God in Christ: The Price and the Prize of the Gospel."[4] At the time, I was really struggling with believing the truths of the gospel as a believer (it was actually while writing this chapter). It was at that appointed time that something he said regarding grace really struck a chord with me. He said, "You know why we're forgiven? So our guilt won't get in the way of us enjoying God. You know why we're vindicated? So our condemnation won't get in the way of us enjoying God!" After hearing this, my mind was blown! I hadn't completely understood that the entire point of being justified for my sins wasn't to beat myself up over my sinful nature and place such a magnified focus on it—rather, the point was to give me freedom from that guilt and self-condemnation that I might "rejoice in hope of the glory of God." God's grace is sufficient to compensate for all of our weaknesses (2 Corinthians 12:9).

Through this grace that He lavishes on us, He consequently gives us permission to live in Him and enjoy Him forever.

Breathe and be reassured that the grace of God covers you every waking hour of every single day. Grace is literally unmerited favor from God. So, if you aren't good enough, strong enough, righteous enough or qualified enough—rejoice! You are the perfect recipient of grace because it is manufactured especially for you, the undeserving one. You are safe in grace's harness!

"You see, at just the right time, when we were still powerless, Christ died for the ungodly. Very rarely will anyone die for a righteous man, though for a good man someone might possibly dare to die. But God demonstrates His own love for us in this: While we were still sinners, Christ died for us."
(Romans 5:6-8, NIV)

RISE & SHINE

"You are the light of the world. A town built on a hill cannot be hidden. Neither do people light a lamp and put it under a bowl. Instead they put it on its stand, and it gives light to everyone in the house. In the same way, let your light shine before others, that they may see your good deeds and glorify your Father in heaven."
(Matthew 5:14-16, NIV)

"For God, who said, 'Let light shine out of darkness,' made his light shine in our hearts to give us the light of the knowledge of God's glory displayed in the face of Christ."
(2 Corinthians 4:6, NIV)

Rise. And. Shine. There's nothing left to be done! In and of ourselves, yes, we are sinners. Yes, we are hopeless. Yes, we are dark. But Christ died—He changed everything! And surely, He didn't stay in the grave. He rose so that we can rise in Him. So shine the light of the gospel to the world. We no longer have to hide from the Light that once exposed us. Instead, we expose ourselves voluntarily, so that Christ may be seen ever so brightly to those who are blinded by darkness. His Light gives us light and we light up the world. What an honor. Shine bright saints. Shine bright.

My name is Charity and I used to be prideful, lustful, idle, cowardly, faithless, irritable—and a host of other evil things. But those things no longer matter, nor do they identify me. When God looks at me, all He sees is the blood of His Son—not my sin, and surely not my shame. I am redeemed. I am accepted. I am loved. That my friend is what makes me good—it wasn't anything that I could have *ever* done to receive such a precious gift. I am because He is, and He is the point of it *all*.

NOTES

Chapter 1: Good Girls

1. Wurmbrand, Richard, *Tortured for Christ* (Bartlesville, OK: Living Sacrifice Book, 1998), p.70.

Chapter 4: Lust

1. Legend, John. "All of Me." 2013.

Chapter 5: Idleness

1. Prison Nation. *National Geographic.* Television.

Chapter 6: Cowardice

1. Beautiful Eulogy. "You Can Save Me." 2013.

2. Bethel Music. "You Make Me Brave." 2014.

Chapter 8: Irritability

1. "Definition of Irritability for Students." Merriam-Webster. Accessed December 19, 2016. https://www.merriam-webster.com/dictionary/irritability.

2. Bridges, Jerry, *Respectable Sins: Confronting the Sins We Tolerate* (Colorado Springs, CO: NavPress, 2007), p.115.

Chapter 9: The Gospel

1. McClister, David. "The Scourging of Jesus." Accessed November/December, 2016. http://www.truthmagazine.com/archives/volume44/v440106010.htm.

2. Davis, C. Truman, "The Passion of Christ from a Medical Point of View" (*Arizona Medicine,* 1965).

3. Henry, Matthew, *Matthew Henry's Concise Commentary on the Whole Bible* (Nashville: Thomas Nelson, 1997), Location 22952.

4. Piper, John. "God in Christ: The Price and the Prize of the Gospel." Desiring God, 10 Nov. 2012, www.desiringgod.org/messages/god-in-christ-the-price-and-the-prize-of-the-gospel.

All Greek/Hebrew words and definitions were attained by using Blue Letter Bible. "Blue Letter Bible." Bible Search and Study Tools - Blue Letter Bible. Accessed December 19, 2016. https://www.blueletterbible.org/.

THANK YOU

I can't believe I'm writing this thank you page. God has been so incredibly gracious and faithful to me it doesn't even make sense. This whole project is legitimately His doing (from conception to completion) and I would be foolish not to thank Him first. Truly, if it wasn't for You Jesus I wouldn't have a reason to write this book at all. I thank You for not only saving me but for granting me the opportunity to share Your glorious gospel. If only *one* person reads this book and is changed as a result, my heart will truly be overjoyed.

To my dear husband, Fenol— I thank you from the bottom of my heart for your relentless encouragement in this. Being in covenant with you is a constant reminder of grace. I couldn't have published this book without you. Thank you for always pushing me to the gospel and showing me my competence in Christ when I wanted to give up. Daddy and Mommy, if it weren't for you I wouldn't be the woman that I am today. You guys have invested so much into raising Whitney and I and we are so blessed to have such awesome parents! You two raised us to the best of your ability in the ways of the Lord. Even though this book showcases my own sinful heart and capacities, I'm grateful to God that He has saved and redeemed me anyhow! I pray that you find peace in knowing that. Whitney (a.k.a. Seester)—I love you so much! Thank you for supporting and praying for me along this journey. Thank you also for allowing me to share some of your business so that God can be glorified ☺. To my Dera home team—thank you everyone for your continual support throughout this process, I love you all so very much, family!

To Karolyne Roberts—thank you, thank you, thank you! You have been so patient with me and helpful throughout this entire process. Thank you for believing in my vision. May you continue spreading the goodness of our God to the world—one book at a time.

A special thank you to Erica Weaver for being my personal theological reviewer. It was vital to me that everything written in this book was theologically sound. Thank you for using your gifts to assist me. Your contribution to this project was truly invaluable.

Simone Martin, thank you love for doing the necessary edits that I desperately needed on my book cover. You're the realest—a true friend and sister, indeed.

To Mrs. Layesha Walton and the L.I.F.T. Mentorship Program—if it wasn't for you, my manuscript would still be on my laptop. Your accountability and encouragement played an integral part in me actually publishing this book. Thank you.

Mrs. Julie Williamson—I can't thank you enough for your support as you were committed to reading my manuscript and making sure everything was doctrinally sound before publishing. Thank you for your willingness to do that so late in the game!

Thank you to Pastor Ron Simmons, Yvette Simmons and my DWAY family! You all have played a major part in my spiritual development over the years and I praise God for you. Thank you also to Pastor Darryl Williamson and my Living Faith Bible Fellowship family for incessantly pouring into me through the faithful preaching and teaching of the Word.

To my Tharren, Cindy, Geornesia, Kierra and Lola—I love all my friends but you all specifically have been incredibly supportive throughout this process. It feels good to know that I have people behind me, praying on my behalf as it relates to this. Thank you for ALWAYS encouraging me—even when the idea of writing a book seemed crazy. You girls have had my back every step of the way. Thank you.

Lastly, to anyone else I might have missed—please charge my head, not my heart! There have been so many individuals who have supported me in a variety of ways. I'm truly blessed to have each and every one of you in my life!

For additional resources and updates from the author please visit charitydera.com

www.ingramcontent.com/pod-product-compliance
Lightning Source LLC
Chambersburg PA
CBHW020615300426
44113CB00007B/651